THE GLASS ELEVATOR

JUTTA DOS SANTOS MIQUELINO

PASSIONPRENEUR®
PUBLISHING

THE
GLASS
ELEVATOR

The ultimate guide for leaders who
believe in Oneness, Collaboration,
and Transformation

JUTTA DOS SANTOS MIQUELINO

PASSIONPRENEUR®
PUBLISHING

THE GLASS ELEVATOR
Copyright © 2024 Jutta dos Santos Miquelino
First published in 2024

Print: 978-1-76124-190-1
E-book: 978-1-76124-192-5
Hardback: 978-1-76124-191-8

Publishing information
Publishing and design facilitated by Passionpreneur Publishing
A division of Passionpreneur Organization Pty Ltd
ABN: 48640637529

Melbourne, VIC | Australia
www.passionpreneurpublishing.com

I dedicate this book to my love and husband Ricardo,
the greatest gift of God in my life,
who inspires me to be magic

and

to my incredible mother Erika, who taught me
being different is wonderful.

CONTENTS

PART III: ORGANIZATIONAL TRANSFORMATION

Boosting Innovation with Collective Intelligence

Appendix

TESTIMONIALS

*T*he *Glass Elevator* by Jutta dos Santos Miquelino marks a turning point in the understanding of modern leadership. Amidst the turbulence of digital upheaval and the challenges of fast-lane management, this book offers a return to the essence of true leadership. Jutta breaks away from the tradition of superficial leadership guides and instead opens the door to a world where leaders create true change through self-reflection and a deep understanding of their role.

My personal experience of working with Jutta has shown that she has the ability to make complex topics accessible and provide inspiring perspectives – a quality that characterizes *The Glass Elevator* through and through. The book is peppered with insights as compelling as the plot twists of a top-rated Netflix series, and it creates a vivid picture of what new leadership looks like in practice.

By introducing the concept of 5D-Leadership, Jutta opens the door to a new dimension of leadership that aims to maximize both individual and collective potential. *The Glass Elevator* goes far beyond traditional leadership teachings and challenges us to explore our inner world in order to more effectively shape our outer realities. It is a call to action for current and future leaders to break free from old patterns and embark on a path of conscious, inclusive, and transformational leadership.

This work is more than a book; it is a compass for those who are ready to embark on the journey to become not only better leaders, but also deeper, more fulfilled human beings. It is an invitation to all to join a movement that is redefining how we lead, work, and live in our age – a movement that aims to leave real change with lasting impact.

— **Prof. Dr. Kai Reinhardt,**
expert on digital transformation and organizational development.
https://www.kaireinhardt.de

* * *

I've known Jutta since the mid-1990s, when she was part of a group of administrative assistants in the marketing department of P&G Prestige Fragrances.

Right from the start, I got to know Jutta as a highly motivated, extremely ambitious bundle of energy who was out to conquer the world. Even though well beyond her job description, she established the concept of cross-functional collaboration as a tool to drive innovation and transparency. This led to the set-up of what became the cross-functional COMET team at P&G ("Customer Oriented Marketing Excellence Team"), aiming to elevate marketing through "outside-in" insights while simultaneously driving customer service to new heights.

Learning from that early experience, Jutta systematically developed this approach as the blueprint for her later roles, replacing traditional hierarchies with an approach centered on collaboration and co-creation across organizational boundaries.

Today, Jutta can look back at an impressive management career in senior global roles at leading blue-chip companies. More importantly, she has established herself as a proven successful and widely recognized entrepreneur and CEO, developing innovative design thinking solutions for core industries and blue-chip companies in Germany and beyond.

In my mind, Jutta is the highly inspirational living proof of what humans can accomplish if they put their mind to it, relentlessly pursuing their goals and ambitions with passion and perseverance.

— **Achim Daub,**

CEO & Board Member OnScent, Former Global President Symrise AG

* * *

Over the many years that I had the pleasure to work with Jutta on various projects, I have always admired her sharp mind, her logical and strategic thinking and problem-solving, and her holistic view of the world.

Jutta has combined all of her wisdom gathered in countless workshops with customers and innovators from around the world and distilled it into *The Glass Elevator*. Applying her ability to break down complex topics into easily understandable bits and drawing comprehensive conclusions from them, Jutta has crafted the con-cept of 5D-Leadership, which should become standard reading for leaders in all fields. Applying the principles of *The Glass Elevator* – not only to team and organizational transformation, but also to personal life – can truly help to start real, sustainable change in the world.

— **Jan Fiedler,**

Digital and VFX Consultant & Tech Enthusiast,

Academy Award® Winner and Emmy Award® Winner for Best Visual Effects

* * *

Jutta and I connected during the pandemic, as we were both working to create happier and more inclusive corporate cultures. Jutta is that rare executive and consultant who puts listening first, above all other tasks, and formulates solutions around the human beings at the core of the company or issue. This leads to extraordinary results! She brings so much outcome-oriented, positive energy to every conversation about business, culture, wellness, relationships, and an array of other topics that I look forward to seeing her name on my calendar every time another meeting is set.

— **Valerie Alexander,**

CEO, Keynote Speaker, Author

https://www.speakhappiness.com/

* * *

I had the pleasure to work together with Jutta for two years in her role as the General Manager Sales Support for Sony Europe Limited,

Germany. Even though she took over the role during a very tough situation for the team (restructure and staff reduction), her excellent skills for team-building and clear communication as well as her great motivational skills made us feel well-prepared throughout that very difficult time.

Furthermore, Jutta implemented a feedback structure across her direct reports which enabled everyone to work hard on their personal development and growth. In particular, in my new role she supported me by giving me great direction on stakeholder communication and structure and increased my self-confidence for my new tasks.

I profoundly recommend Jutta as a highly motivated, goal-oriented, well-structured, and efficient business and team leader.

— **Franziska Belz,**
Project Manager Fulfilment Development IKEA,
former Logistics Manager Sony Europe, German Branch

* * *

The coaching experience with Jutta felt like a stepping-stone which I needed to unlock a gate for a 10x fast-forward personal transformation. Even one year after we ended the coaching, I am still exploring and applying the methods and tools which she has handed me and still feel like I am growing every day.

Jutta has a very structured approach; every session is designed to your specific situation and needs. Through her extensive experience, ranging from international fast-moving consumer goods conglomerates and tech-oriented large companies to German-based traditional mid-cap firms and startups, Jutta has a story to tell and provides the insight to address your challenges. With her empathy, positive spirit, and holistic approach to helping you help yourself – which spans way beyond simple business coaching – you will not only strongly gain confidence but also excel.

— **Josephine Ackerman,**
Head of Strategy & Brand, SCHUFA Holding AG

* * *

Jutta not only combines a holistic personal development with leadership knowledge and business experience. Jutta sets individual transformation and growth as the core of any success story in leadership and business. I have the privilege to actually explore the personal transformation journey Jutta is describing and I am even more blessed to be accompanied and guided by her.

Jutta completely embodies a value-based and empathetic leadership approach that is manifesting in two basic competencies: mindful listening and true interest in the personal growth of the individual Jutta is interacting with. Jutta is not looking at you, she is looking into you, helping you to discover your inner drivers and to identify your better self. I have never met a person that is as present, content and settled in the here and now, while – at the same time – looking open-minded and visionary into an even brighter future.

If you want it or not, Jutta will let you grow, so you better embrace this gift directly ...

— **Matthias Kellersohn,**
CEO & Managing Director Henkelhausen GmbH & Co. KG

Jutta is a real powerhouse. Her visionary mind paired with her generous heart and action-oriented approach makes her a real role model for me. Watching her develop over the last two years has been nothing short of astonishing. Since our first meeting at a *Mindvalley* event in Berlin, we have met at least once a month for our "Goddesses" lunch and I have witnessed her immense growth first-hand. I experienced one laser coaching session with her which was exceptional; she seamlessly blended warmth and sharp analysis and got me straight to the point. Every interaction with Jutta leaves a spark and motivates me to be better.

Within her book *The Glass Elevator*, she showcases her transformative leadership philosophy and ignites a passionate pursuit of personal and professional growth through a new area of leadership. Her 5D-Leadership method boldly challenges boundaries to achieve holistic transformation and connectedness.

— **Sarah Perings,**

Training Manager Carl Zeiss Meditec AG

* * *

Jutta is one of those people who are changing the world. She is a woman with an open heart and mind who not only talks about her values but embodies them with dedication and conviction. Her book *The Glass Elevator* redefines the essence of leadership in the contemporary era. It shows the pathway for how leadership can be used to help people become more profound, happy, and fulfilled human beings – which, in my eyes, is crucial for changing our planet for the better.

I sincerely hope that many leaders will read this book and live up to its values, using their impact and power for good.

— **Hanna Oberkersch,**

Dipl.-Ing. Architect, Fine Artist, Serial Entrepreneur

https://hannaoberkersch.com/en/

* * *

Do we need another book on leadership? All I know is: THIS book is much needed. It will help leaders unleash their own full potential and that of those they lead. Everyone is looking for that one method or strategy that brings you 5% or 10% more ...

Jutta's approach leverages the hidden potentials and resources within people, leading to unimaginable outcomes. Jutta is my spirit animal when it comes to power, courage, and fun. I admire her ability to express boldness and tenderness simultaneously, and to make people around her shine.

— **Friederike von Benten (Sadhana),**

Founder of Aloha Vita Coaching and The Bliss Party, Keynote Speaker, Author

https://alohavita.com/

* * *

I had the distinct pleasure of working with Jutta on various projects, including for the Swiss Future Institute AI Future Council, where she shared her invaluable insights on diverse dimensions of thought leadership. Jutta brings an unparalleled spirit combined with a depth of knowledge, a natural and engaging leadership style, and a consulting innovation expertise that is completely different from those I have known before. This made me curious from the very beginning when I met her. Her engaging style, coupled with her energetic, wise manner, made the conversation captivating to listen to, follow, and reflect on. She is a true source of inspiration, and I am grateful to have her in the AI Future Council and as a valuable business partner.

— **Katrin J. Yuan,**

Chair of the AI Future Council, Swiss Future Institute, CEO and Board Member

https://www.futureinstitute.ch/

* * *

I'll never forget listening to Jutta's inspiring story, when I told her, "You have a book in you, and you can inspire many." I'm so glad to have sparked the creation of this book. Reading it fills me with pride, knowing I was the catalyst for its conception.

Jutta's concept of 5D-Leadership is not only unique but also profound, reflecting her extensive experience and distinctive perspective.

Highly recommended for new-age leaders.

— **Pegah Gol,**

Board Member & Investor, AI Talent Platform Author, Executive Career Coach

* * *

To be in Jutta's presence is to be inspired. Her energy, her charisma, her courage and her experience make me believe that the necessary changes in our corporate structures are indeed possible. And her book reflects those very qualities. Jutta's book is a must-read for anyone in a leadership position. From fostering innovation to creating a culture of continuous improvement, this book provides a roadmap for success in today's rapidly changing world.

— **Jasmina Hirschmann,**
Co-Founder DODEKA, Trauma and Mindset Coach
https://www.dodeka-themindfulcollective.com/

* * *

Jutta is a STAR and has the knowledge, talent, and passion to make a true difference for so many. I admire her courage and her strength. Jutta and her values represent the future, the way it could be, and I certainly hope it will be for my grandchildren and great-grandchildren. Love, respect, diversity, and compassion. That is what makes life worthwhile and happy. Planet Earth is so lucky to have Jutta as resident to teach us a better way.

— **Mary Carethers,**
President & CEO Innovation Connections LLC,
former global Senior Vice-President R&D Procter & Gamble

FOREWORD

The *Glass Elevator* by Jutta dos Santos Miquelino is a pioneering work that acknowledges the shift in our environment – more fluid, ambivalent, and brittle – and pairs it with a more dynamic, personal, and holistic approach to leadership. As a Professor of Digital Transformation and a professional dealing with digital transformation since 2017, I have witnessed first-hand the pivotal role leadership approaches play in cultural change, which in turn drives – or blocks – transformation.

Jutta's holistic view of 5D-Leadership laid out in Part I *Personal Transformation* particularly excels in that it doesn't make leaders suffer but enables them to grow – in all dimensions. It's hard to become a great leader, and it is more customary to do so by sacrificing yourself. This, however, leads to your leadership being short-lived.

Jutta shows another way. A way of being a great leader and growing your own personality at the same time. It involves a journey of self-discovery and self-actualization, urging leaders to engage deeply with their values, beliefs, and purposes. From experience,

I can tell you how rewarding – and fun – this process is. Above that, the personal transformation of leaders she writes about is deeply necessary – I have seen too many good leaders fail because they could not sustain themselves.

In Part II of this book, *Team Transformation*, Jutta's concept of leadership consists of making significant impacts on human wellbeing and organizational health – at the same time. Jutta discusses the importance of this *"human-centered business transformation"*, where the focus shifts from processes and systems to the people who make up the organization, fostering a culture that supports personal and collective growth. This resonates with me on a very deep level, having left the corporate world to grow freely, as well as having founded my first company to enable the team to grow fully and my second to motivate our customers' employees to grow. I am fighting the same battles as Jutta does. That's why I am deeply grateful for these exquisitely crafted chapters. It should be mandatory reading for all business and strategy consultants, on par with Excel and presentation skills.

Jutta's thesis in Part III, *Organizational Transformation*, is that we need a learning culture that embraces continuous improvement and adaptability as core organizational values. It should be KNOWN by all by now, but it is still being DONE by only a handful of companies.

That's why I am a particular fan of her practical approach, in which we are kindred spirits. She intersperses practical tools, real-world examples, and actionable steps to help leaders implement her concepts in their professional lives. Each chapter concludes with exercises and reflections designed to assist readers in applying the principles of 5D-Leadership to their own situations.

For true leaders, in my experience, leadership improvements cannot come about without spiritual growth. That's why Jutta's book is so important. It is a blueprint for building a more compassionate, understanding, and sustainable world through enlightened leadership practices.

— **Prof. Dr. Katja Nettesheim,**
CEO & Managing Director Culcha
https://www.culcha.com/

BEHIND THE WORDS

My Journey as an Author

"I believe ambition is not a dirty word. It's just believing in yourself and your abilities. Imagine this. What would happen if we were all brave enough to believe in our own ability, to be a little bit more ambitious? I think the world would change."

— REESE WITHERSPOON

First of May, first day in my new management role. Shortly before 9 a.m., I step through the open front door into the impressive reception hall of the Sony Centre at Potsdamer Platz in Berlin. Thanks to the impressive glass façade, it's as bright and sunny inside as it is outside. Well-dressed people on their way to their offices or hurrying to the cafeteria smile at me as I pass by. Then my gaze falls on a Japanese businessman who greets me silently with his eyes, nodding his head as he ascends swiftly in a glass elevator from the basement. I look after him in amazement and ask the friendly lady at the reception desk, who just handed over my Sony ID card to me, where the elevator has just come from. *"The entrance to the VIP parking is down there,"* she explains kindly. *"Mr. Asami-san takes the elevator directly from the underground carpark to the top management floor."* Wow! At that moment, I suddenly saw myself taking this VIP elevator to my office on the top management level and smiled at the idea.

I liked it! One day, I decided, I will take this glass elevator to my office on the top floor for the executive managers.

At first, I moved into the open-plan office, leading a team of four in my middle management role. But only two-and-a-half years later, the time had come: I was appointed to the Executive team and my dream came true, now leading a unit of nearly one hundred, as the first woman in the history of Sony CE Germany reaching that top management level. A dream with many facets, as it turned out. I enjoyed the magnificent views over Berlin's picturesque Tiergarten every day as I took the VIP elevator to my own office and thanked God, my source, and my spiritual guides that had supported me to get there. My rise to the executive management level was not only a climb up the corporate ladder; it inspired me to believe in transformation, proving I could combine growth and conscious living on my own terms with professional success.

When did I start feeling so deeply connected to my source that I believed magic things like becoming the first woman in Sony's top-management level could happen to me? At the age of twenty-five, I experienced a profound shift in consciousness through spending weeks in almost complete silence, caused by a loss of my voice diagnosed as laryngitis. I was overworked, having spent weeks preparing for a big international marketing event at Procter & Gamble on top of my duties with too many calls and excessive pressure through last-minute changes.

I felt disrupted; newly single, I had separated from my partner after five years of a loving relationship, without really being able to express why I had to leave him, which hurt him a lot. The illness expressed how I felt: speechless. I moved into my new apartment, with hardly any furniture – and no internet, TV, or telephone, as the building was still being finished.

Warned by my doctor of potential cancer caused by misuse of my vocal cords, I vowed to keep silent while I was signed off from work for a month. People facing a crisis often embody the resilience of a phoenix rising from the ashes. Alone, I embraced the opportunity for a fresh start, sparking my personal and professional rebirth by seeking books on awareness, loving relationships, and mastering life and happiness. This uncomfortable retreat became my new awakening, and in this quietude my purpose geminated: to meld spirituality with technology and career, as well as to disrupt traditional leadership concepts by focusing on personal growth and wholeness.

When Silence Inspires

The silence allowed me to inhale the books and reflect on them for hours during the day.

> *"Those who look outward dream.*
> *Those who look inward awaken!"*

was the message of C.G. Jung. It dawned on me – there exists a higher consciousness that can unite our minds and bring humanity together. We create the love for ourselves and others in ourselves. This realization was followed by many books of the Dalai Lama and Ken Wilber's *Paths to Self*, which shaped my understanding of the concepts of *"Transcendence"* and *"Oneness"* at that time.

Leadership isn't a crown we wear; it's the path we carve with empathy, innovation, and a relentless pursuit of collective elevation. Conscious business isn't merely about profit margins and market shares; it's about shaping an enterprise soulful at its core, resilient in its pursuit, and captivating in its reach. Melding purpose with strategic planning, the human potential with the heartbeat of technology, and the ambition to elevate as many as possible with a unified consciousness, revealing that we are all one and live in alignment with nature.

The Path to Transformation

My career path from personal assistant at P&G to marketing manager with responsibility for millions of dollars, and breaking through the glass ceiling to the executive floor years later, was no walk in the park – more a roller-coaster ride, marked by many setbacks and moments of deep despair. I like adventures and extreme sports; I've dropped out of airplanes, and I like to come back to myself on the yoga mat. It's a good place to recalibrate through career fluctuations, and I'll explain why breath is all you need in the last chapter. Because as Yogananda says,

"Your trials have not come to punish you,
but to awaken you!"

Today, it's become my life's mission to support executive leaders in raising their individual awareness and that of their organization and in strengthening cooperation, mutual trust, *Wertschätzung* (appreciation), as well as a sense of mutual responsibility. With a higher level of awareness, it's much easier for us to leverage the full potential of people and technology with the goal of developing a healthy economy for a healthier planet. Happiness at the workplace is the magic potion for raising people's productivity; that's a fact. Organizations don't only need to be more productive – they also need to be innovative and creative while becoming learning organizations, where employees inspire each other and collaborate. That's a path of transformation which isn't easy to walk for today's leaders. Together with my love and life partner Ricardo, the founder and co-CEO of ... *and dos Santos*, we're committed to using our think tank of international thought leaders to solve these complex challenges in organizations with collective intelligence, while developing transformative solutions for a better tomorrow.

The client lists of ... *and dos Santos* includes Europe's Top 100 companies across various industries including Deutsche Bank, Deutsche Bahn, L'Oréal, Unilever, Walt Disney, and Zeiss.

Our holistic approach helps to recode a company's DNA to a new level and supports activating people on a mental, a spiritual, and an energetic level. We provide access to a collective of outstanding experts and are linking internal with extraordinary external expertise. We help organizations accelerate their cultural and digital transformation and meet the major challenges of our time, such as a diverse workforce, a shortage of skilled workers, and the high speed of technical innovation and change regarding the consciousness and beliefs of employees. Our projects have been honored with the global Bold Award for the *"Future of Work"*.

As a conscious strategy consultant, I believe the best strategy you can have for your business is to focus on *people*, supporting them to develop their full potential. Technology – especially artificial intelligence – will enable you to create highly profitable business models, which is why you need people who embrace AI and create profitable solutions in their respective areas of responsibility. They'll only do that wholeheartedly if they trust your leadership, and they'll only trust you to the fullest if you embrace humanity with all kinds of diversity it offers. To do so, you must embrace your human self to the fullest first; and you will need all your feminine and masculine powers to pull this off.

THE CONCEPT OF 5D-LEADERSHIP

In this book, I'll share a concept I call 5D-Leadership, aiming to dedicate your leadership skills to serving humanity with the ultimate aim of reaching *Oneness Consciousness*.

Why should I serve humanity, you may ask?

You can decide to serve for money, or impact, or power. It doesn't matter how much money or impact or power you gain, nothing will fulfill you.

You'll experience abundance, wholeness, love, inner peace, and happiness if you dedicate your life to helping humanity and being of divine service for the greater good of all.

Read this book if you want to give yourself permission to open up to greater levels of leadership and impact on others without authority. Our business is still small, but our hearts at ... *and dos Santos* are open and fulfilled. Becoming a 5D-Leader can be the path to your inner and outer growth. You have everything you need within you to become the best version of yourself and be a visionary leader on your own terms. This means it doesn't matter where your starting point as a leader is, whether you're still a student or assistant, executive or CEO, founder or entrepreneur. If you enjoy being in business, love elevating your team and organization to a higher level, and innovate and transform to keep pace with technological and demographic change, you're in the right place. I'll help you surrender to your inner truth and experience an inspiring life on your terms. Your life and your business will profit when you pursue wholeness – and as a result, humanity profits, too.

A Passion for Wholehearted Engagement

According to Gallup, in the *2023 State of the Global Workplace* report, low employee engagement costs the global economy an estimated US$8.8 trillion. That's 9% of global GDP, enough to make the difference between success and failure for humanity. Poor management leads to lost profits, but it also leads to miserable lives. Having a job you hate is worse than being unemployed and those negative emotions end up at home, impacting your relationships and the whole family. If you're not thriving at work, you're unlikely to be thriving at life. Please don't wait for others to do this work for you and create a fulfilling job. Do it yourself. Become the best leader of your life and of your team you can imagine, step by step.

When you feel blocked or not fully engaged in your role, this book can help you. I'll offer you guidance on how you can reconnect your values with your work, or help you decide to make a relevant change. In an exponentially changing world, we need trustful collaboration within the power of the collective. This requires leaders who allow an open, two-way dialogue with their people, and who are willing to learn from them as well. Harnessing collective intelligence and elevating human consciousness are key pillars for 21st-century businesses as they enable organizations to tackle the speed of change.

You aren't born with leadership skills; unfortunately, neither are the skills of how to raise your consciousness or master your life taught at schools. On top, you need to reach wholeness and happiness first before you can teach it effectively to others. Teilhard de Chardin said:

"We are not human beings having a spiritual experience;
we are spiritual beings having a human experience."

We need more leaders that live in harmony with their human experience, that respect and lovingly embrace their body and mind while deeply connecting with their spirit, and that are aware of the different dimensions of reality. I'll explain this in the next chapters, reducing this overwhelming complexity of different consciousness models to five levels to aid understanding. This is an invitation to a journey of self-exploration that will never stop once started. All you need is to be committed and decide to define your leadership role as your vehicle for growth.

Turn the page and explore how you can access the luminous path to 5D-Leadership, overcoming scarcity or duality, becoming fully self-actualized and empowered to transcend.

THE LUMINOUS PATH TO 5D-LEADERSHIP

Why we need to reconnect our souls with
our business to achieve happiness,
transformation, and extraordinary
growth in the workplace

*"All people have an ocean of achievement
inside themselves just waiting to escape."*

— SHEIKH MOHAMMED BIN RASHID AL MAKTOUM

You are a leader, and leaders help others to flourish.
We humans thrive in life only when we live it wholeheartedly,
and we spend most of our lives at work. We shouldn't experience inspiration and fulfilment only in our few hours of free time; our
workplaces must provide space for it. You are responsible for driving

innovation, whether in management, production, service, or any other area. Since the evolution of data and technology are accelerating with incredible speed, you must learn to cope with these fast developments, adapt them, and create better results through AI or any other type of technology. You need open-minded people in your team who embrace change without any fear, ready to step into uncertainty. But our mind prefers to stay in the comfort zone just to keep us safe.

Your role as a leader now comes into play because you're the beginning of any change. Our reality has unlimited dimensions; there's a universal truth which you realize when you go inside and remember who you are. Wholeness, a fulfilled life, is the potential reward if you align your soul with your purpose, your actions, and your business, thus helping create meaningful work for others. With time, this will allow you to achieve extraordinary goals and higher levels of impact, while experiencing great joy every day in doing so. You can achieve your goals with hard work, or with love, grace, and flow if you're in alignment.

The five dimensions of reality I'm describing in the book are a way to explain levels of consciousness to make them easier to grasp, starting with a very low level when in survival mode up to the highest – the *Oneness Consciousness*. However, these dimensions aren't easy to reach. Those who feel a bit closer to a higher dimension dedicate their energy to helping others rise and shine in life. You chose to read this book to elevate not only yourself as a leader, but also your inner circle (family and friends), your outer circle (employees, colleagues, community, business partners), and more. When you grow, others will grow with you.

Embrace 5D-Leadership to unite your inner purpose with your professional role, at whatever level you currently are. You'll find concepts about creating a workplace that breathes innovation and satisfaction.

This book equips you with practical tools to raise your leadership consciousness and encourages a holistic approach to business. You'll learn to harness collective intelligence, tapping into a wealth of internal and external resources for breakthrough innovations. Continual learning and self-awareness are pivotal, leading to a unified consciousness that aligns with your business goals, ultimately benefiting humanity.

LACK OF EMPLOYEE ENGAGEMENT SLOWS INNOVATION

The current engagement levels of workers demand a rapid leadership change. According to Gallup, the global employee engagement rate in 2022 was 23%, with 18% of employees actively disengaged. In Europe, Germany has an even lower figure at 16%, France is at 7%, and Italy is at 5% of engaged employees. We needn't be surprised that European companies have become less innovative overall. At the same time, there are best practice examples that achieve 72% engagement. It's possible to motivate employees and keep them happy and highly engaged. We must stop the brain drain effect, as too many of the EU's best researchers and innovators leave for countries where conditions are more favorable.

The causes of the *"decline in innovation"* are diverse and complex. We need to help ourselves, not wait for help. We need to change our inner attitude, our inner dissatisfaction with what currently is, and consider how to significantly increase our motivation, curiosity, and openness to collaboration again. Let's think about how to get out of this crisis and create a better business world from the inside to the outside. Every person who's gone through a deep crisis knows what a great opportunity it offers. Every leader should seize this great opportunity now – so when you see your company is in crisis or you feel it personally, decide to be a phoenix, the beautiful mystical bird symbolizing rebirth, renewal, and resurrection. His death and subsequent rebirth represent the cyclical nature of life and the eternal nature of the soul. The phoenix also represents the triumph of life, the ability to overcome adversity and rise again.

We need a new way of meaningful leadership, one that whole-heartedly empowers the leader from within. Because the moment you disconnect yourself from your leadership role's purpose, you automatically distrust your people. The moment you distrust your people, you stifle their innovation and start to become a controller, which increases mistrust. Good leaders hold people accountable, and accountability begins with you.

Reconnect your soul with your business, bring your head and your heart in alignment with a positive vibe. The people around you will feel the change – and most of all, you'll feel it. In the process, you'll experience a new level of happiness, energy, power, and true connectedness.

On this journey to a new way of leadership that comes from your heart and your soul – from the growing awareness that when you reconnect throughout the day with your own source of inspiration, you're using it as an impetus for inspired activities – you'll unfurl the best in you. Work becomes easier, motivation is increased, and the everyday experience of work is much more enjoyable. You can act with a stronger attitude, taking a stand with grace. Your soul is pure light, but you need to nurture it so that it fully shines through you. A stronger soul connection will strengthen your intuition and allow you to unleash more creativity to approach problems, instead of just using logic (which is of course necessary, as is rationality).

However, you'll know exactly what to do in moments when logic no longer serves you.

The Glass Elevator will elevate you to access higher levels of your consciousness. You can only increase awareness level by level, through an individual learning process; the path to achieving your personal goal is also an individual one. Respecting your individuality is the key.

As a leader, are you happy and proud of the business world we've created so far? No? **Be the change you want to see in the world** and take action to unfurl the best in yourself.

CHAPTER OVERVIEW

This book is divided into three parts:

PART I – PERSONAL TRANSFORMATION:

Stepping into 5D-Leadership

PART II – TEAM TRANSFORMATION:

Elevating 5D-Leadership Consciousness

PART III – ORGANIZATIONAL TRANSFORMATION:

Boosting Innovation with Collective Intelligence

PART I:
STEPPING INTO 5D-LEADERSHIP

consists of the following three chapters. It guides you through different dimensions of your reality, including how you can evolve as a leader by dedicating your life to limitless personal growth and contributing to the rise of humanity towards a *Oneness Consciousness* – a world that allows rational and mindful business growth.

Chapter 1: The Activation – Ignite Your 5D-Leadership

You will explore the five dimensions of reality and what effect they have on your life experience. I'll offer tools to help you ignite your power as a 5D-Leader, describing the advantages of vertical growth and how you can dissolve inner blocks that keep you from evolving faster.

Chapter 2: Cultivating Purpose-Driven 5D-Leadership

This chapter will help you identify your Leadership Purpose, including how to align it with the values and goals of your current role. You'll learn about the *Life Diamond*, the tool that allows you to unfold in all areas of your life and combine your goals in work and life in the best way.

Chapter 3: Experiencing Your True Growth Path

We'll go deeper into the methods and steps for vertical development. First, I'll explain the *Feedback & Growth Cycle*, and second, I'll reveal how you can get out of the downward spiral of negative emotions and transform them through awareness and alchemy into positive energy.

PART II:
ELEVATING 5D-LEADERSHIP CONSCIOUSNESS

offers you methods to enable a positive change in awareness among your team, colleagues, and stakeholders, thus increasing innovation as well as stronger collaboration and coherence.

Chapter 4: Human-Centered Business Transformation

Have you ever taken a human-centered perspective on your business? Instead of looking at products, processes, or value chains, we'll examine the soul, heartbeat, and higher consciousness of your business, as it's an organization sustained by divine people.

Chapter 5: Nurturing a Diverse Culture of Excellence

We'll dive into how to nurture a diverse culture of excellence through activating the male and female energies in your team (as every human keeps both energies inside), and why this approach supports you in driving innovation, creativity, and performance.

Chapter 6: Elevating Extraordinary Team Spirit

You'll gain insights and learn about methods of how to measure and elevate an extraordinary team spirit, and why focusing on human needs and energy frequency are keys to creating better results.

PART III:

BOOSTING INNOVATION WITH COLLECTIVE INTELLIGENCE

will explain how you can design a *collective genius* to tackle complex challenges in your company. You'll learn a new process covering the development and implementation of disruptive innovations, and how to ignite the joy of limitless learning to keep the 5D-Leadership spark alive.

Chapter 7: The Symphony of Thought Leaders

Why is it possible to gain a deeper understanding of your own business when you create a *collective genius* with the help of extraordinary thought leaders? We'll dive into this method, including how to stimulate both sides of the human brain to accelerate your team's innovation and expansion capacity.

Chapter 8: Design Thinking for a Better Tomorrow

This will show you how to activate the collective growth zone of your team members by igniting a design thinking process and the use of the *collective genius*.

Chapter 9: The Learning Curve

We'll dig deeper into the *Learning Process* and explain why establishing a limitless learning culture is the prerequisite for any organization that wants to thrive in the future.

Chapter 10: Sustaining the Spark

Finally, we'll put a spotlight on the fact that each new level you'll experience on your growth path will challenge you again, from the very moment you've just achieved it.

Every chapter has a clear focus, and all chapters build on each other. I'll use real-world examples and case studies that illustrate the concept of 5D-Leadership and offer specific, actionable steps that help you implement these principles in your professional and private life, including exercises, checklists, and reflection questions. I also employ visual aids and illustrations to make these sometimes-complex ideas easier to grasp.

Online Experience

For people who want a deeper dive into the concepts in this book, I'll share additional resources along the way – please check out the links at the Sources section and the Recommendations at the end. You'll find interactive elements like self-assessments, worksheets, meditations, further information, and activations on the webpage for this book: glasselevator.me

BEFORE WE GO ON

"Philanthropy is not about helping others, it's about helping yourself. When you change, the world changes."

This quote by Jack Ma, the Founder of ALIBABA, states a simple truth. When you develop yourself as a conscious 5D-Leader, people will become inspired by you, support you, and help you ensure that your vision comes true.

With time, you'll evolve faster, set more ambitious goals, and realize that your outer reality reflects the inner frequencies of your consciousness and subconsciousness that you can't easily control, but can learn to influence. The world needs peace, and we as humans have to accelerate the growth of our human consciousness to a level where we feel connected and willing to dedicate our lives to keeping others and our planet healthy. When we're capable of stopping the war inside of ourselves, we'll stop the wars on the outside.

It all starts with you, so ask yourself: **Are you open to a new way of soul-led leadership?**

PART I

STEPPING INTO 5D-LEADERSHIP

PERSONAL TRANSFORMATION

CHAPTER 1

THE ACTIVATION – IGNITE YOUR 5D-LEADERSHIP

Setting the intention to lead with positive impact will positively impact your life

"This game of money, this game of leadership, this game of living our best life ever, is a game of frequency.
Your frequency is your currency. When you feel deflated and not enough, that affects your frequency, and you are not able to own your power. If you are in a state of power and your truth, you'll attract and manifest in your 3D reality what you desire. We are all here to leave the planet as a better place, so find your purpose, your truth and ignite your 5D powerplay; this is a journey that never stops."

— REGAN HILLYER,
World's #1 Manifestation Teacher

5D-Leadership goes beyond leading a team to success. It's about being in harmony with yourself, acting and reacting in full awareness, with integrity and authenticity. What we call matter in the universe is energy, and every human is surrounded by and reflects an energetic field. Once you realize that your reality reflects the frequencies you create inside, and that you can influence your outer reality through the way you act on and react to situations, you'll want to increase your frequency while learning to use and understand your emotions, as well as doing the alchemy to transfer any negative energy into a positive energy in motion. Why? Because you can create the best life you can imagine if you become the best and most powerful version of yourself. And there's no need to become your own boss or create your own business – you can of course unleash yourself in your current role, too!

The powerplay, as Regan Hillyer describes it above, is not power that pushes others down; it's one directed by humility. One that aligns you with your inner truth. If you choose to walk this path and take full responsibility for your actions and reactions, doing the inner work every day to expand your awareness and dedicate your life to inner growth, you'll unleash the ultimate leader in you. In the process, you'll positively influence not only yourself, but also your family, your friends, your colleagues, your organization, and beyond.

The personal advantages of choosing the path of evolving your conscious awareness and vertically growing to reach 5D-Leadership are indescribable.

Why do more and more 5D-Leaders, like Satya Nadella (Microsoft), Arianna Huffington, Marc Benioff (Salesforce), and Oprah Winfrey (Harpo Productions) step away from traditional leadership models that focus on service in terms of stakeholders' interests, to reach a new perspective based on spirituality and planetary service?

Because the world needs change.

2023 was the hottest year on record, we have an escalating polarization of conflicts, our world is in a culture war, and we collectively create results that nobody wants. Leaders need to lead the change and release their ego to become eco, one system, *Oneness Consciousness*.

Why five dimensions? The five levels of reality I describe, from Survival State to a Dualistic Stage, from Self-Actualization towards Self-Transcendence up to *Oneness Consciousness*, aren't a scientific proven model – they're a simplified, abstract view of our unlimited reality.

By the end of this chapter, you'll understand what the path to 5D-Leadership is all about, know how you can step into your individual power through practice, and understand the process of how to increase your levels of awareness influencing your current reality.

There are more and more leaders dedicating themselves to serving unity and peace.

"I enjoy the world of business and the process of problem solving … I don't just want to make money. I want to add value and feel as though I am making a contribution to the world around me."

— JEFF WEINER,
Executive Chairman
and former CEO of LinkedIn

For me, one of the most powerful examples of a master in 5D-Leadership who accelerated the metamorphosis of a business and achieved exponential growth is Jeff Weiner. As CEO of LinkedIn, he's propelled his platform to reach more than 900 million users and 75 million organizations. Jeff started at LinkedIn in 2008 (with only approximately 33 million users at that time) and the company witnessed a tenfold increase in revenue four years after his appointment. He also played an instrumental role in LinkedIn's acquisition by Microsoft for $26 billion in 2016.

Jeff's superpower lies in anchoring a culture of compassion and performance. He promoted focus on team performance and personal growth, conscious responsibility, inclusivity, and empathy. His three management pillars are awareness, synthesis, and inspiration. Most importantly, this phenomenal rise is based on fundamental business ethics, as well as his belief that you can't be a great leader unless you lead spiritually.

In numerous podcasts and articles, Jeff writes about his spiritual evolution and enlightenment. He even offers a free course on LinkedIn, "Managing Compassionately", to educate leaders who accept their imperfections, raise their levels of awareness, and achieve profit through abundance rather than scarcity.

These creative leaders enjoy the process of problem-solving. Leaders that are more interested in growing, expanding, creating, and giving than taking from others. And leaders who are more driven by the sustainable people-centered values they create than simply beating a competitor. Jeff has embarked on the path to *Oneness Consciousness*. He meditates daily, and his life's vision is to increase the awareness of our society. He continues to share his important leadership message to humanity across multiple channels.

Conscious 5D-Leadership suits leaders who wish to use their personal power to do good for humanity. As a conscious leader, being of service to others by helping them succeed and thrive is your goal. How do you differentiate 5D-Leaders from mainly profit-driven ones?

· **5D-Leadership emphasizes a higher state of consciousness,** where leaders aren't only self-aware but also acutely aware of their role in a larger interconnected reality. Traditional leadership often focuses on practical skills and outcomes without necessarily delving into the leader's inner state or sense of interconnectedness with the universe.

· **5D-Leadership integrates spiritual principles and practices,** such as meditation and mindfulness, into the leadership journey. Traditional leadership models may incorporate elements of personal development, but don't typically include spirituality as a component of leadership. Rational leaders don't consider their energetic impact or vibrational state as factors in their effectiveness.

· **5D-Leadership takes a holistic view. By considering the wellbeing of the leader,** the team, the organization, and the wider community, it seeks to balance personal growth with organizational goals, whereas traditional leadership models may prioritize the organization's needs (often at the expense of personal development).

Activating your 5D-Leadership starts with understanding the different levels and multi-dimensional concept of personal growth, from the 1st to the 5th dimension. Reflect on this concept, thinking about where you find yourself and what resonates with you.

THE FIVE DIMENSIONS OF REALITY

There are many models and frameworks analyzing human consciousness, many describing different states of human development. When I first came access Ken Wilber's Integral Theory many years ago, I found it incredibly eye-opening how complex our being is and how much there is to learn.

Much more popular is Frederic Laloux's book *Reinventing Organizations*, where the author links Ken Wilber's stages of consciousness with the maturity of organizations. If you'd like to dig deeper, a great comparison of different human consciousness and behavior models is also offered by scientist Clare W. Graves in his *Spiral Dynamics map*, which has been compared with the models and maps of other leading researchers. All these models – whether they use six, seven, eight, or more stages – recognize that human development is a complex process involving multiple dimensions of experience, including cognitive, emotional, social, and spiritual. I love analyzing complex theories and narrowing them down pragmatically to make them simple and easier to grasp. That's why my model explaining the overall idea behind 5D-Leadership is reduced to five dimensions.

1st Dimension of Reality – "Survival and Reactionary Living"

The 1st dimension is the most basic level of existence, where you operate primarily on instinct and are primarily focused on meeting your basic survival needs such as food, water, shelter, and safety. Life at this stage is often characterized by reactivity, where you respond instinctively to your environment and circumstances, and there's little room for self-reflection or growth. While you're in survival mode, you're in constant need of money, or food, or shelter. Your body and mind are focused on mere survival, and you're looking for allies to help you escape this unpleasant experience. You often feel victimized because of the circumstances you're in. All humans want to be significant. One way to gain significance fast, even when you're poor, is via terror and violence. You're significant in a second with a gun in your hand forcing somebody else to go down on their knees in front of your eyes, or if you force them to give you the money you need. "No poverty" is the first of the UN's 17 Sustainable Development Goals (SDGs), as it's essential to allow

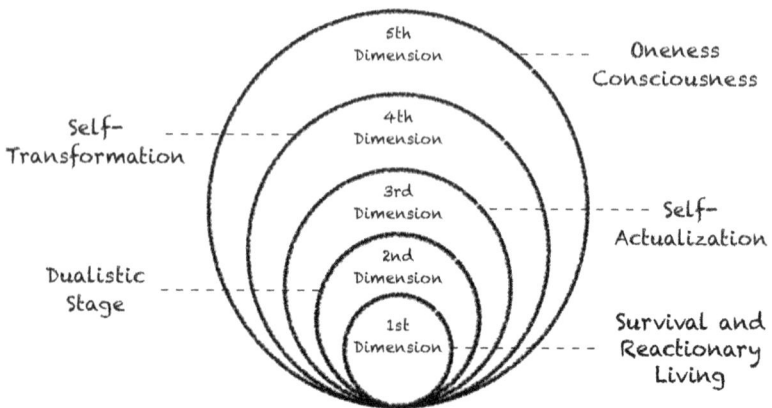

humans to experience happiness and evolve. Unlike in Maslow's pyramid of needs, I included experiencing love and belonging as part of this 1st dimension because humans that feel disconnected from others and don't experience belonging are usually depressed and not capable of contributing to humanity in a positive way. Connecting with others is elemental to our survival. This first stage is a dimension of reality where people suffer during their everyday existence. We must create a world that allows all humans to evolve without survival fears and achieving our 17 SDGs is the prerequisite for it. The goals are set to be reached in 2030, but we're a long way from achieving them.

2nd Dimension of Reality – "Dualistic Stage"

In this next level, you start to engage with the world in more complex ways. You're capable of experiencing a range of emotions, and your actions are driven not only by survival but also by pleasure and pain, reward and punishment, right and wrong. Life becomes more than just surviving; it's also about thriving within social norms and structures. You develop self-esteem and your ego dominates.

When you're living in this "dualistic" state of consciousness, you view things in terms of binary opposites like right/wrong, good/bad, etc. Therefore, this stage is characterized by a strong identification with the ego and the physical world.

You often experience the world emotionally as a feeling of separation from the unified field of consciousness; your reality is emotionally distorted with low vibrations. You face a lot of scarcity; often feeling anger, you use your energy to push through actions without first connecting to your soul or higher self. This kind of push energy is often described as *"male energy"*. I'll come to this in more detail in

Chapter 5, but it's active in all humans and not dependent on the sex. You win over others through dominance or tricks. As a result, life is often unfair. You work hard to achieve results, or are on a treadmill, preferring to solve disagreements through force, blaming others, or even more harmful methods. Your vibrations are still too low to attract higher-vibrating people who support you unconditionally. Think about your relationships and how you treat your loved ones, your family, or even your colleagues and employees. Do you use your dominance to get what you want? This may make you feel like a winner, but it's a result of treating life as a win or lose game which is no fun to play in a world where we're all connected and create ripple effects with our actions. If you exude dominance, you don't feel guided and protected by a higher consciousness, and you often feel alone – but that's your decision. Simply put, if you act like a jackass, you'll be surrounded by jackasses. They may be very rich and powerful, but they stay jackasses – while you have no access to true love, connectedness, and happiness. Act with love, and love will be all around you most of the time.

3rd Dimension of Reality – "Self-Actualization"

As a reader of this book, I assume you're experiencing the 3rd or 4th Dimensions of Reality. **The 3rd Dimension is the level of Self-Actualization. You start to focus on personal growth and realize your own potential. You seek experiences that foster growth and self-fulfillment.** You pursue your passions, seek authentic relationships, and strive to understand your place in the world. Personal values and internal motivations guide your actions, rather than external rewards or societal expectations. This stage corresponds to Maslow's 5th level of hierarchy (self-actualization), which was the peak when the pyramid was first published. Living on this level is already a great achievement of personal growth. You master your career, your key relationships, your money, your community.

However, you're not yet fully dedicated to service for others, and you feel not fully aligned with your purpose in life. You still compare yourself with others around you who might have "more" money, love, success, or impact. There's a way to live and wake up in the morning with a happy heart, an open mind, gratitude and a sense of knowing what to do next, and to experience more magic and joy than you can think of if you experience life at the 4th Dimension. But you understand you have access to choice, so you don't react to your thoughts; you're aware you can choose better thoughts from a higher version of you, you may already work with vision boards and mindfulness practices, and you're open to self-development work.

4th Dimension of Reality – "Self-Transformation"

At this level, you move beyond personal needs and seek to contribute to something larger than yourself. You experience a deep sense of connectedness with the rest of the world. Your perspective shifts from a self-centered view to a broader, interconnected perspective. You find fulfillment in serving others, contributing to the community, and working toward a greater good. **At this stage, you seek to step into your discomfort zone (often during the day, as you're fully aware that this is your growth zone). You see yourself recognizing your limiting thought patterns, and you catch them in an attempt to release them.** You've transcended your ego and accepted the role that you play in your ecosystem and the world, however small it is. That was a key learning experience for me; it's more relevant to feel from the inside that you're on this level than comparing your achievements with those on the outside. Because not everybody is made to run a business like Jeff Weiner, every life path and purpose is different. Some people are more flexible than others, and can therefore grow much faster and gain more impact. To reach fulfilment by experiencing wholeness and abundance, you have to set up to this 4th Dimension of conscious awareness – the level of reality where your most important needs are met and where you feel your energetic transformation. Happiness starts the day you wake up and open your eyes. You consciously use your sleeping time to solve problems, trusting your intuition that it's working for you. You're dedicated to putting your body in the best possible state to create the energy you need to create your best life. You practice cleaning your body and mind, creating space for new thoughts, new codes, and higher vibrations. You feel that your body is a vessel for a loving and inspired mind, dedicated to growth.

The transition from the lowest to the highest dimensions isn't a one-step process for most people, and it won't be for you. The process may take many, many years. Remember, these stages aren't always linear; they can be cyclical or even concurrent. It's also worth noting that reaching higher dimensions doesn't mean abandoning or transcending the lower ones. Individuals still have basic needs, experience a range of emotions, and have personal goals even as they strive for self-transcendence. It's your decision to walk the path to your illumination.

Dedicate your life to reaching 5D-Leadership, and it will help you realign with your higher ground whenever something pushes you out of your comfort zone. You can learn to activate and use your personal alchemy to transform negative experiences into positive energy for growth and transformation. And once you've learned this, you'll seek and find your community that continuously supports your growth.

5th Dimension of Reality – "Oneness Consciousness"

This stage or dimension could be viewed as a deepening or an expansion of self-transformation, where you not only feel connected to the world around you but also feel in tune with the flow of life and the universe. **You feel connected on a quantum level, as a creator of your life's reality. At this level, you might experience a profound sense of unity with all of existence, where the boundaries between self and other, between you and the universe, start to blur. You accept what happens to you as a gift to evolve and further expand your consciousness.** You may perceive an increase in synchronicities or meaningful coincidences, feeling as though you're "in the right place at the right time" more frequently. Some people describe this as an experience of "flow" on a cosmic scale, where life seems to unfold with ease, and they feel in alignment with their purpose and their universal experience. Others describe it as a state of heightened intuition or a sense of "knowing" that goes beyond logic and reason. You're in service to others, using the income you generate to gain a higher positive impact in return. Sound like a great idea to reach the 5th Dimension? **What does it take to ascend?**

How to Accelerate Your Personal Growth

An inspired leader like Jeff Weiner lives and acts on a high frequency. In exchange, he receives the abundance and growth he creates. He loves to solve problems; he loves to create great results; and he loves to be an inspiration for others to grow. Success is an inner game, because you define what success is – nobody else. If you listen to your heart and soul, the answer will be: You want to create *impact*, not money. You want to add value and feel as though you're contributing to the world around you. Success isn't about having money in the bank. This makes you rich, yet many rich people feel poor. Accept that your mind lives only in the present. If you feel weak, hurt, or humiliated, you won't be able to act easily and openly with others. Instead, you'll lead through commanding and controlling – and as we all know, this doesn't really work.

Whatever others say to you, and regardless of how they make you feel, reflect on it and recalibrate your feelings. That's what we call alchemy. By accepting any emotional state you're experiencing, you can learn from it and grow beyond it.

5D-Leadership means you can manage whatever's thrown at you, finding the stillness and connectedness not to react dramatically but with ease. Understand that you're powerful, in the deep sense of truly knowing your worth not from your ego, but from your true being. Let's start with a task that focuses on your current self-thoughts about your leadership skills and capacity. Your inner voice when you're in a stressful situation is often full of worry. Expressing thoughts like *"I can't do this"*, *"I don't know how to deal with this"*, and *"Why does this happen to me?"* are normal. Our self-talk influences our actions and reactions, and it takes work to listen to yourself and replace negativity with better thoughts and self-talk. Negative beliefs are the ones that are limiting your actions, forcing you to react in a certain way.

Exercise to Ignite Your 5D-Leadership

Step 1: Dimensional Self-Awareness

Become aware of the five dimensions of reality and commit to your growth. Ask yourself: **Where are you at? In what dimensions do you feel comfortable? How does the 5th dimension** *Oneness Consciousness* **resonate with you?**

Have you ever experienced this deep moment of true connection with everything, while you were in nature, or meditating, or deeply in love with somebody and trusted in oneness? The tasks are joyful if you're fully self-aware. Get raw and real about your inner truth – starting now, take a pen and paper and start journaling.

Step 2: Leadership Affirmation

List the top fifty reasons why you're a great leader. Write them down, let it flow. If you stop after nine, ten, or twenty-five reasons, you're limiting your self-worth. Become aware of yourself and understand this is the basis of your very own leadership level. Think about when you achieved as a leader what you thought was impossible. If you tend to skip this, you're not open to experimentation or are afraid to face your blocks. That's normal. This isn't a race or competition. It's just a reflection of where you're currently at. The task feels great if you just do it and free your mind. Enjoy remembering why you're a brilliant leader. Search deep down in your heart and stay connected with your inner truth, believing what you write.

Step 3: Power Dynamics Reflection

Analyze your leadership power in all areas where you feel weak. When and how do you consciously (or, much more likely, unconsciously) give your personal power away to others? When do you feel weak or victimized? Become aware when you lose your energy. That's real, and uncomfortable, work. Take your time and listen to yourself. Go into detail when you reflect on this. Feel the responsibility of what's happening in your life and how you react in situations when you feel weak with your partner, your colleagues, your boss, your kids. Bring this into awareness from your unconscious. Create a routine with this task, staying aware while you do it. Pinpoint during each day when you lose power or let others dominate you. There's an opportunity to gain another chance to react differently.

Standing Strong Against Humiliation

In hierarchical cultures, it's quite common to experience humiliation during your career. It's important to not take this personally, but instead insist on being respected. When I was Head of Operations at Sony and a member of the Executive team, this was a challenge – not only for me, but also for many male top managers. It was the first time in the history of the subsidiary that they had to deal with a woman at this level. A new Japanese colleague, now Head of Marketing, introduced himself to me in a first meeting and immediately brought along a multi-faceted report on our supply chain situation. He asked me line by line and column by column what it was all about; in most cases, I was able to answer him well. But at one point I faltered, because I wasn't sure what he meant. Then he lost his attitude, exploded, and shouted at me in a deep and harrowing samurai voice, the kind I only knew from the movies like Tom Cruise's *The Last Samurai*: "*You are Sales*

Operations Head; you have to know that!" I was shocked by this sudden violent emotional eruption. As his negative energy blocked me completely, I remained silent and looked downwards. Then I apologized, assuring him that I'd find out exactly what the requested column in the report meant. But I was also seething, because shouting at me like that was outrageous and unacceptable.

Immediately wishing to learn how to deal with such a rude attitude, I asked my assistant to arrange appointments with this new Head of Marketing. Unfortunately, I still didn't manage to react to his shouting in a confident manner at the second meeting, where he shouted me into submission again over another report. But at the third meeting, when he thought he had a reason to humiliate me, I stood my ground. After his usual yelling, I asked him why he wasn't talking to me in a reasonable voice. After all, I said, I want to help him and answer his questions – but that would require him to speak to me respectfully, in a normal voice. He was speechless and became downright meek. He hadn't expected a confident counter-attack from me. From that meeting onwards, he never shouted at me again. On the contrary, I became a kind of confidante for him, and he repeatedly sought my advice.

It was my positive self-talk that I deserve respect for, along with my determination to endure his uncomfortable and humiliating shouting until I was able to react with confidence. Other colleagues reacted to this rude man different-ly. When a colleague quit her role at Sony, she told me: *"I couldn't respect his bad behavior as my boss anymore."* You can quit, or you can create your respect.

Step 4: Daily Empowerment Practice

Create your daily routine to get into your leadership power zone. When something is thrown at you and you feel negative emotions, meditate, have a walk in nature, or practice gratitude and inspiration. You'll find some guided meditations in the online 5D-Leadership section of this book glasselevator.me/5D-Leadership. You can find many other meditations in apps like *Headspace* or *Calm*. Find the spiritual teacher that guides you best. Access your powerful self and fall in love with that self. This will make you a better leader. We're all human; we feel weak, have bad days, and experience humiliations. But how you deal with these emotions makes the crucial difference. Ask yourself *why* you feel weak. Use every evening to reflect on how you can react better to situations – with more gratitude, more self-respect, more self-love, more compassion, or more authority.

Key Reasons Why People Struggle with Stepping Into Higher Dimensions of Reality

· Your surroundings will tell you this is bullshit and vertical growth doesn't work.

"Your brain is like tofu.
It becomes whatever you marinate it in."

So says Dr. Sara Al Madani, an Emirati serial entrepreneur and tech innovator. We must become the gatekeepers of our brain and take full responsibility for our body's energy management; this way, we can create a better tomorrow for ourselves and others. You may have heard the rule that the five people around you reflect where you are in life.

Change the people around you if you feel they don't energize you positively. After all, there's no way to thrive and grow when others pull you down. Don't be afraid of change or emptiness; it creates space for new beginnings.

· **You can't find the time to enter silence and stillness while continuing to be reactive.** We all have only twenty-four hours during a day, but we can influence how to spend them, at least for several minutes. Start with five minutes every day for thirty days. Afterwards, reflect on how you feel different. Join a personal growth community of your choice and talk about your blocks and limitations with others who've shared the same struggle. You'll transform fastest when you're witnessed.

· **You don't believe that *Oneness Consciousness* exists.** The concept is found in many religious and spiritual traditions, including Hinduism (as in Advaita Vedanta), Buddhism (the concept of interconnectedness in the doctrine of dependent origination), Sufism, Christian mysticism, and various indigenous spiritualities. There is a growing scientific interest in understanding oneness, especially in fields like psychology or neurology, exploring how certain brain states correlate with experiences of oneness and how these experiences affect mental health and the perceptions of the world. For example, Eric Van Lente's study about *"Understanding the Nature of Oneness Experience"* uses collective intelligence methods to understand the nature of oneness, employing an interactive management process to generate oneness-related experience. Stay curious, keep discovering, and you may tap into a new dimension of knowing.

Remember Who You Really Are

Now you understand the five different dimensions of reality, and you started your growth path by identifying a minimum of fifty reasons why you're a great leader. If your list isn't long enough yet, remember that negative self-talk is a key reason why you're stuck in your current reality. Learn to listen to your inner voice and catch the negative thoughts, reflecting on how they serve you and whether there's something to learn. Keep curious and seek answers, including: **Who am I, really?** Learn more about how you can access your subconscious mind, then recode it. **What are my hidden treasures? What wants to be revealed?** Take the time to learn more about yourself, observe when you give your power away, including to whom and why you're doing it. Maybe it's your family background and feeling like being a victim is a *"normal"* attitude for centuries in your family – whatever it is, bring it into the light.

Summary of How to Activate Your 5D-Leadership

1. Dimensional Self-Awareness

Recognize and embrace the multi-dimensional nature of personal growth. Commit to ascending through the five dimensions of reality, from basic survival to *Oneness Consciousness*, by consciously engaging in your own development journey.

2. Leadership Affirmation

List at least fifty qualities that affirm your leadership prowess. This exercise isn't just about self-appreciation, but also about recognizing and overcoming the self-imposed limits on your self-worth and leadership capacity.

3. Power Dynamics Reflection

Examine the instances where you cede your power, whether knowingly or unknowingly. Understand the triggers that make you feel weak or victimized, then develop strategies to reclaim your strength and stand firm in your leadership role.

4. Daily Empowerment Practice

Establish a routine that helps you stay centered and powerful each day. Whether through meditation, nature walks, or reflective practices, ensure you nurture gratitude, inspiration, and a strong sense of self. Use the routine to cultivate resilience and a more profound leadership presence. For more advice and meditations, or if you like to use the 5D-Leadership self-assessment tool, check out the online section glasselevator.me/5D-Leadership. In the next chapter, you'll connect this personal transformational process with your current leadership role. It's about cultivating your purpose-driven transformation, aligning your values with those of your organization, and diving deeper into how you connect your soul with business to lead from your heart, powered by your inner truth.

CHAPTER 2

CULTIVATING PURPOSE-DRIVEN 5D-LEADERSHIP

Your world will change when you connect
your soul with your business

*"Everyone has been made for some particular work,
and the desire for that work has been put in every heart."*

— RUMI

When you don't connect with your job on a deeper level, when you spend hours every day being someone who functions well in your role, but is concealing the real you, you waste your precious lifetime. I also spent too many years of my life at this level, until I understood how to connect the different worlds. I felt disconnected during the day, but still told myself

"I have my spirituality", which was nothing but an escape. You feel wholeness when you're in alignment, happy and content in the now. And since I know both sides of business well – the corporate and the entrepreneurial – I assure you it doesn't matter whether you serve your own business or a bigger company. In both roles, you can be in full alignment or not. You need to do the inner work in any case.

The Significance of Purpose and Dedication

When I didn't identify with the values and purpose of my role, I was on a treadmill with low vibes. It was hard to get up in the morning and commute to work, hard to get my to-do list together, and even harder ticking off the tasks. I was running away from my emails, I participated in meetings without listening, I was happy to distract myself with browsing the internet, checking social media, or having a much longer coffee break than I needed. I had no energy to do any sport before or after work – and when I was home, I put on the TV to consume even more. These phases were the worst in my life. I was in an emotional downward spiral, disconnected from my soul. My mind rotated around how I could find an escape from my job, so I booked a series of holidays and at least enjoyed traveling. My world changed only when I consciously started to reconnect my soul with the role I was serving.

Crisis is an Invitation to Growth

Your soul's calling doesn't just knock on your door and say *"hello"*. Instead, you need to peel it off layer by layer. Connecting your soul with your current role will heighten your intuition and inspiration.

You'll create a deeper desire for the work that's been put into your heart, as Rumi said, when you allow it to unfold. Allow any crisis to help you expand your awareness. For instance, when recession is knocking on the door, leaders must help organizations shrink to fit. Most leaders are afraid of restructuring, as it's always a painful process to lead through, but it's an ideal zone for personal growth.

A Tsunami Unleashed my Leadership Purpose

When I was the Head of Operations at Sony in 2011, Japan was hit by a disastrous earthquake, followed by the tsunami and the nuclear reactor catastrophe in Fukushima. Almost 500,000 people fled the triple disaster, and more than 160,000 had to be permanently resettled. The production capacity of Sony was drastically hit. Soon after the disaster, Sony had to reconstruct its business, deciding immediately to release 5,000 employees across Europe. One of the famous *"Big Three"* strategic consultancy management firms was called to help Sony go on without these 5,000 souls.

I received the order to significantly downsize the Operations team, fast. I was shocked of course, even horrified. Because I was new to my executive role, I had a leadership coach by my side. I told him about the task lying ahead of me and he said slowly, *"You will be the bitch of the company, so you better create yourself a cozy home"*. I shared that with my husband and immediately ordered a small fireplace for our apartment, to create a warm and cozy place that would await me if a day turned out to be too tough. I meditated, promising myself to deliver the best restructuring project in the most humane way I was capable of. I loved Sony and its people, and was grateful for this new role. Having started with just four people two years ago, this was my third promotion in three years. I now oversaw a team of nearly 100 people across seven departments. I also felt connected with my Executive team members and didn't want to disappoint them, as I was grateful for their trust in my leadership qualities. I spent many evenings in front of my new fireplace thinking of what to do next, because restructuring is always a painful process. But my team was strong and upright, and we went through the crisis together, keeping our spirits high and hugging each other when needed.

I managed the change by putting the focus on the people. When I received the official restructuring plan from Sony's European management, which had been set up with the strategic consultancy and explained in their detailed restructuring plan (named after a flower, for some reason), I was firstly shocked about the rigidness of the restructuring. After examining the details, I doubted it could work (superficially maybe, but not in detail).

The new organizational chart was based on assumptions about how processes were organized in Germany, in line with the European or UK model. However, because the special features of the German organization that had grown up over the years couldn't simply be glossed over, a new bottom-up plan was needed. The clearly defined KPIs for the restructuring could be achieved, but in a different way, which first had to be defined.

Together with my team, I prepared an overview of the daily tasks our people fulfilled within their units, which we needed to redesign the new organizational structure. The setup of this task overview took all my department managers weeks to compile, but we got transparency and understood the interdependencies between the different roles much better. Based on this in-depth understanding, we could begin redesigning the new organizational structure.

During my next 1:1 with my boss, I shared my doubts and the research I'd done on operations. Insistently, I asked my CEO not to go ahead with the so-called *"flower"* plan. Instead, I suggested we stick to the KPIs we had to achieve, but then take a few more weeks to work out a solution that would guarantee a solid business result. He spent a night with my research and overview, then called the top European Management team. After intense discussions, I got the green light. I'd gained their trust by consistently achieving or exceeding my KPIs in former assignments, but I also had to deliver. Fortunately, I was fully committed.

There was a lot of imperfection in my leadership. I made painful mistakes, and learned to apologize openly for these. Luckily, being vulnerable builds an incredible amount of trust.

In short, we managed the restructuring and exceeded some of our operational KPIs with a smaller team. Germany won the Excellent Management Performance Award in 2012 as the best-performing country, driven by the excellence of the whole organization and the well-performing Operations team that was still undergoing heavy reconstruction. We were proud.

By the end of 2014, I decided to leave Sony together with the CEO who'd hired me five years earlier. When I left, my team informed me that the personal growth they achieved through this intense time was the greatest gift that I'd given them. Many found this experience of being open, positive, energized, human-centered, and vulnerable quite new. Connecting my soul with the restructuring tasks helped me follow my intuition to change the official plan, which was disruptive and risky, opposing the European status quo. My positive energy attracted people, who supported me to help make it happen.

PRINCIPLES FOR PURPOSE-DRIVEN 5D-LEADERSHIP

Here are the five principles I recommend to guide you towards a truly inspired leadership:

1. Purpose Alignment

Make your purpose your priority by serving a company which supports the prosperity of humanity and is dedicated to creating a more sustainable future. Only then will you find it easy to align your role with your inner purpose. We're here on this planet to create a better future; we're not here to make it a bad place in the universe. You'll find purposeful companies in all areas, whether it's insurance, energy, transportation, the food industry, or finance. Check if there's clear dedication to creating a positive impact. Provided your company has a pro-humanity vision, study it and ask yourself:

- Why did I choose this company to be my employer?

- What are the "Wow" moments I'm experiencing here with my colleagues?

- What purpose does our company fulfill?

- What is the company's main vision – the one that we strive for?

- What are the key goals to reach that vision?

Write down the purpose of your company. If there's already an existing statement, rewrite it in your own words to make sure you really find the true meaning behind it.

As a next step, articulate the personal purpose of your role:

- What do I want to leave behind in the next twelve months?

- How will the people around me think about me now?

- What stories should people tell about me when I leave?

- How can I positively influence my colleagues?

- What shift in their energy do I want to create?

Ask yourself these questions deeply, then listen to your answers from your spiritual core and take the time to write them down. Done? Wonderful! Now, bring these two purposeful descriptions together – your personal purpose, and the organizational purpose. When you're clear about your own purpose, you can align your actions, decisions, and strategies accordingly. Your purpose doesn't need to save the world or have an impact on the whole society; instead, start with your team. Read your purpose statement every day before work, and with time you'll find it easier to act with the good intentions you see in yourself.. You'll be happier about the good results you're achieving than ever before. Any kind of failure will simply represent another type of learning. Even if they are painful, mistakes are good for growth.

2. Values Integration

Your values are what define you and are linked with your soul. My personal values are transformation, collaboration, excellence, love, and oneness. In my first job with P&G, I was participating in a leadership training program, where we had to define our values and bring them together with the company's. P&G's values are integrity, leadership, ownership, passion for winning, and trust. These are strong values and high standards; at that time, I already loved bringing my own values in harmony with my role. You see, these values don't contradict, but complement each other and provide guidance. Even in the small role of a personal assistant, my intention was to act in accordance with my core values.

Are you able to list the values of your company by heart, or do you have to look them up first? If so, why don't you care about them? Do you believe that these are just empty phrases, because you see that the people around you don't live by them? Start with yourself! When I interview top management teams, I always ask them how they interpret the company's values for their own role. In 95% of the interviews, I receive answers like: "Your question indicates that I took the time to reflect on the company's values and how they touch me and how I want to act on them accordingly, right?" "Exactly, that's what I was asking for" is my answer. Then usually comes a pause. And this pause usually comes not from the newbies, but very often from leaders who serve for many years. They had no idea. Your life is short, so make it significant and consciously provide value for others.

Understand the values of your company, then reflect on, interpret, and live by them. In the next steps, write down what kind of actions others will identify as those you'll be able to bring to life.

If trust is a value, **how do your colleagues feel that you're 100% trustworthy? What needs to change if you're going to eliminate all doubts?**

Dig deeply, because the answer is always inside of you. If you need help defining how to transfer your values into actions, please check glasselevator.me/5D-Leadership to find an inspiring reflective activation.

3. Visionary 5D-Leadership

What future reality do you want to experience in your organization? How do you get there? As a 5D-Leader, you recognize the importance of understanding your inspirational role and your responsibilities within your organization. When you've written down the actions that unite your values with the company's, and then begin to practice them, this will cause a big shift from the beginning. Connect these values and action principles with your ambition, vision, and targets. By being clear about your inspirational role, you can effectively contribute to the organization's overall vision and mission while increasing happiness and trust. Be a human-centered leader. You'll focus on growth, collaboration, solving problems, and profit, coupled with the ambition to give your company an even stronger positive global impact. By being loaded with positive emotions and energy about your purpose, you'll thrive. Choose purposeful role models that inspire you deeply, break your old thought patterns and seek new horizons.

"Spread love everywhere you go. Let no one ever come to you without leaving happier."

— MOTHER THERESA

4. Energy and Frequency Synergy

Success is an inner game, and your frequency is a fundamental tool in achieving your goals. Being committed to getting better every day and leaving people happier after they've talked to you – or at least inspiring a smile and sharing positive energy in the room – is an essential step in increasing productivity and strengthening collaboration. I'm sure you've found yourself in the *"command and control"* style many times when you want to push through your perspective and make others move immediately in your chosen direction. Yet leading with authority, negativity, and aggression causes resistance. On the other hand, learning to inspire with positive energy and vision will help you become even more effective. The best part is, you'll attract other leaders around you with your positive and energetic vibrations, even those in higher management roles. They'll become your buddies, your mentors, standing by your side during the bad times.

When you choose your organizational surroundings based on your purpose and values, you'll find other leaders that are here for the same reason as you are. Trust your instincts and sense their positive energy, even if you don't know them. Connect, then make them your allies. If you fail to find peers you want to connect with on your level, reach higher, but don't focus only on those above you. Of course, you can vibrate with anyone – for example, connect with the cleaning lady who shares her smile, or the happy clerk behind the counter. But successful people are often generous and like to act as mentors, so ask for their support. Manage your micro-moments, expand your positive frequency, and regularly check in with yourself:

· Did I activate happiness and spread good vibes today?

· How did I delegate my tasks –
engagingly, or in a "command and control" style?

Write in your journal regularly, ideally every evening. Note down the moments you were grateful, too. By doing this, you'll increase your positive awareness of your leadership style and become happier in the day ahead.

5. Creating Magic Moments

Do you believe you can create magic? Does magic happen to you in your life? It happens to me, because I *believe* I can create magic. Magic happens when a client calls me out of the blue, asking me to run a valuable and challenging project with them. Magic happens when I'm working on a challenging project, and my team members come up with a fantastic solution I'd never thought of. Magic is when my husband surprises me with a quote like *"It's not always right to be right"*, accompanied with a smile. My husband loves to be right and usually corrects me immediately if I make even the smallest mistake. Being married to a perfectionist is no walk in the park, but he knows himself well enough to joke about it – that's a magical moment for me.

There are the big magic moments in your life – when you met your beloved partner for the first time, or you finished the first marathon, climbed that mountain you were dreaming of ... or maybe even published your first book. But I'm talking about the very *small* moments, those you can proactively create – when you buy flowers for your partner out of the blue, for example – and those instant inspirations you can receive through your awareness. I taught myself to consciously create magic moments, noting that where my focus goes, my energy flows When you meet your team, think: **How can**

I make this moment more magic? For example, you might start the meeting by telling a funny story, sharing a joke, or giving someone a compliment to make them feel just great.

Gratitude for being is a healing process. How often do you pause during the day, and allow yourself to simply feel this?

High performance is a result of high vibrational energy, not only hours of hard work. So turn your hard work into play, considering how to contribute your inner best. You'll find the five-step process to purposeful leadership summarized in the illustration below.

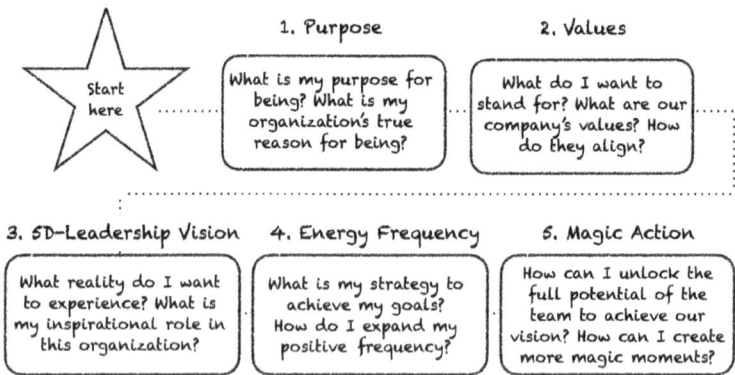

A Great Example of Purpose-Driven 5D-Leadership

Patagonia, a company renowned for its outdoor clothing and gear, has long stood as a beacon of purpose-driven leadership. Its founder, Yvon Chouinard, has instilled a philosophy where the love of nature and a feeling of responsibility towards the environment are at the core of the business strategy. In the early 2010s, Patagonia faced a paradox: Its success was leading to increased production, which inherently conflicted with its mission to "cause no unnecessary harm". In short, the company's growth trajectory was at odds with its environmental ethos. Leaders at Patagonia had to reconcile these competing forces without compromising their foundational values.

At this crossroads, Patagonia realized that the company's purpose goes far beyond profit. It's rooted in the preservation of the natural world. This clear understanding of their 'why' enabled Patagonia to make decisions that may seem counterintuitive to traditional business models. For example, the company's infamous "Don't Buy This Jacket" campaign urged consumers to reconsider potential purchases, reflecting their commitment to reducing environmental impact, even at the cost of potential sales. Patagonia's values of integrity, environmentalism, and responsibility are visibly woven into the fabric of its operations. This was demonstrated when the company transitioned to using 100% organic cotton, despite the financial and logistical hurdles, because it aligned with their environmental commitment. The leaders of Patagonia serve as exemplars of what I call 5D-Leadership. They inspire through taking action, leading environmental initiatives, and advocating for conservation. The company's venture fund, Tin Shed Ventures, supports environmentally and socially responsible startups, further extending its vision.

The leaders maintain a high vibrational frequency that resonates with like-minded consumers, employees, and communities. Their commitment to the environment creates a strong, authentic connection with stakeholders, drawing customers who share their values and fostering a loyal community. Patagonia has created *"magic"* by turning consumers into activists. Their initiatives, such as the *"Action Works"* platform, empower individuals to engage in environmental activism, thereby amplifying their impact far beyond the commercial sphere. The alignment of values and actions, coupled with purpose-driven leadership, has not only solidified Patagonia's brand loyalty but also established it as a leader in corporate responsibility. The company's success and influence in environmental activism exemplify how a business can thrive financially while making a positive impact on the world.

Patagonia's journey is a testament to the transformative power of 5D-Leadership, cultivating meaningful and impactful direction in professional endeavors for a healthier planet. It's a clarion call for leaders to introspect and align personal and organizational values, thereby creating a legacy that transcends the bottom line.

What if You're Unable to Align Your Values with Your Company's?

Not every company is as dedicated to its values as Patagonia, who decided to take values-based action and received high engagement from their employees as well as their customers as a result. What if you realize you're unable to align your values with your current company? Congratulations on your newfound awareness! No need to take disruptive actions – simply think deeper, and make sure you stay engaged even in difficult times. Don't let any thought crises negatively affect you; instead, use it as a gateway to learn something new about yourself. Accept the new situation, thinking about how you could constructively react to a value-driven perspective. When your frequency is low, meditate, journal, stretch, go for a walk, start breathing. In other words, reconnect. Your vision of what to do next is inside of you.

Choices shape our lives. You can choose a life of ease and comfort, or pursue one of service and adventure. Be the change you want to see in the world and become a self-directed leader.

Summary of the Five Key Steps to Align Your Purpose:

Step 1: Purpose Alignment

Define and resonate with your core purpose, ensuring it's in sync with your organization's mission. This alignment guides your actions and contributes to a cohesive goal.

Step 2: Values Integration

Identify your personal values and compare them with those of your organization. Aim to harmonize these values and actively embody them in your professional conduct.

Step 3: Visionary 5D-Leadership

Embrace your role as a transformative leader by establishing a clear vision. Understand how you can inspire change and growth within your organization and your team.

Step 4: Energy and Frequency Synergy

Cultivate a positive energy frequency by connecting with individuals and environments that elevate your spirit and amplify your impact.

Step 5: Creating Magic Moments

Strive to foster moments that leave a lasting, positive imprint on others, essentially weaving *"magic"* into the fabric of everyday interactions. **Why will this intensive examination of yourself and your values bring about a significant change in your life? Because it allows you to demonstrate your higher self-worth.**

Make your deeper connection with your soul visible and tangible for others, and you'll experience change and transformation in your everyday work, because you'll create more value for others through this inner choice. With the increase in your professional quality, your quality of life will increase; living and acting according to your values invites similar values into your life. Imagine you extend this value-driven approach to your whole life. On that note, the next chapter is all about wholeness.

CHAPTER 3

EXPERIENCING YOUR TRUE GROWTH PATH

Why you need imagination, desire, and failure to reach wholeness

"We do not need magic to change the world, we carry all the power we need inside ourselves already: we have the power to imagine better."

— J. K. ROWLING

The award-winning author of the *Harry Potter* series, J.K. Rowling, managed to escape poverty to become one of the world's highest-paid authors. What's her magic potion? In her famous Harvard Commencement speech, she emphasizes appreciating the power of imagination, experiencing failure, valuing friendship, and following her dreams as the essence of her success. Whether it's Rowling, Steve Jobs, or Oprah Winfrey, their diverse commencement speeches still share common themes: realize your dreams, learn from failure, follow your heart, use your imagination and intuition, and serve a greater good.

Why do so many of us put this advice aside and continue to focus solely on our career, making money, and avoiding failure? Maybe the idea of experiencing failure sounds uninviting: J. K. Rowling was *"jobless, a lone parent, and as poor as it is possible to be in modern Britain, without being homeless"*. This is a starting point nobody wants to share – after all, who wants to experience poverty? As Rowling reveals, however:

> *"You might never fail on the scale I did, but some failure in life is inevitable. It is impossible to live without failing at something, unless you live so cautiously that you might as well not have lived at all, in which case you fail by default."*

Design and Plan Your Life Like You Do in Business

We don't dare to live our dreams, as we too often feel we're not good enough; however, we *all* have the power to imagine a better life, even if we don't often focus on it. In my corporate career, we spent every year with strategic planning sessions, breaking down in great detail how we want to achieve our goals, what type of campaigns would best support each product launch, and how we should address our customers. The budget meetings (e.g. at Sony) took weeks of preparation, as well as a whole week of discussion. But too many businesspeople don't invest their time imagining and planning their private life with the same precision. I consider at length how I can deepen my family relationships, or how I can intensify my loving relationship with my beloved husband. I plan adventures and exciting holidays in great detail. I also develop a clear strategy to express my intellect, preparing a *"must read"* list of books or selecting training courses to improve my skills one after the other. I spend hours creating mind maps and vision boards to define who I want to become next, and I just love to update them every year and look back on what dreams came true and which are still open.

Unleash Your Human Potential
as a Leader to Allow Others to Do the Same

5D-Leaders evolve in all areas of life. Our lives are multi-dimensional – people want to live theirs to the fullest, and so do you. When you evolve as a person and unfold the best version of yourself, your quality of life and professional standing grow as well. All facets of life are interconnected; when you're unhappy in your love life, for example, you're not the best leader of others. Making every facet of your *"diamond of life"* shine takes commitment, the time to imagine and plan your desires, and the belief that you're worthy of receiving your dreams. When you start every morning spending five minutes imagining the great day you're about to have and the future you desire, completing this simple task can motivate you to achieve better results.

In this chapter, you'll learn to connect deeper with your desires, imagination, and commitment to live your best life ever and make your *"life diamond"* shine brighter. I'll share the tools to help you activate your imagination, understand your emotional spirals more deeply, and explain the growth cycle that will help you master your emotions. Through these actions, you'll accelerate the manifestation of your dream life and lay the foundations of 5D-Leadership.

THE LIFE DIAMOND

Think about all the different facets of your life and how they're interconnected. Most people focus on career, partnership, and family, yet neglect their health or fail to imagine how to make their existing relationships deeper, lovelier, or more significant. Your quality and impact as a leader are boosted when your overall quality of life improves. Here are eleven categories to consider, with limitless opportunities to evolve in all of them:

- Health
- Emotions
- Relationships
- Love Life

- Spirituality
- Passion
- Intellect
- Career

- Lifestyle
- Wealth
- Contribution

Unfortunately, we don't learn how to explore and unfold our passions at school, let alone how to lead happy and fulfilling relationships, manage our finances, or increase our wealth. After finishing school, we instead spend all our lives figuring out how to earn money and find our dream partner. Later in our career, when we may have got married, we have many things to do and learn – but by that stage, there's no time for learning how to design our life, develop great relationships, become masters in lovemaking, shape our personality, define our contribution to society, or deepen our spirituality.

Health

Emotions

Relationships

Love life

Intellect

Spirituality

Passion

Lifestyle

Career

Wealth

Contribution

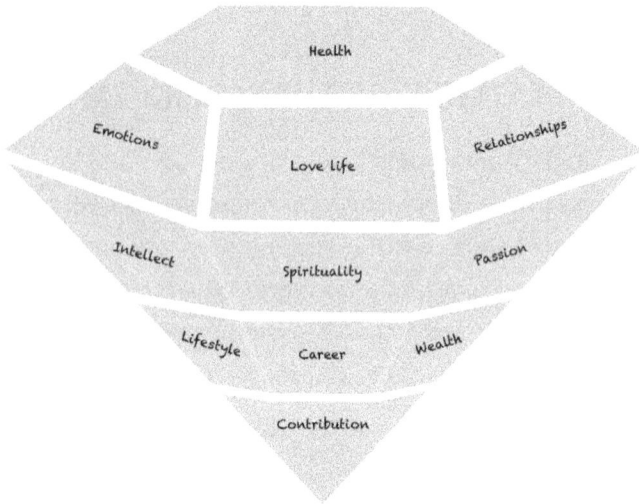

Step 1: Inspect all Facets of Your Life Diamond

Whenever you're aiming to improve any aspect of business, you usually start with performing an analysis and checking the status quo. When you want to improve your life, start with the status quo. Go through all eleven facets of the diamond above. **Does your multi-dimensional life already sparkle and shine in all areas, or do some of them need a rub and a polish?** Give each facet a ranking from 1 (low) to 10 (superb), then ask yourself: **How do I feel about myself within this facet?**

After that, ask yourself: **How do I desire to feel in this area?** Write it all down, taking the time to find out where you're currently at. Be honest with yourself, even when you feel your results are disappointingly low in some areas. When your love life needs an upgrade, that's OK. You can decide to become the most loving partner in the world. There's no right or wrong when you start – instead, just be clear and happy with your shining focus areas.

After you've completed the first assessment and understand where you're at with all eleven facets of your *Life Diamond*, delve a bit deeper into each facet to learn more about your desires:

· **What do I want to experience?**
  Imagine how this desired experience feels, tastes, looks, smells, etc.

· **Why do I want to experience it?**
  Is this a desire of your soul, or your ego?

· **How do I need to think differently about myself to deserve it?**
  Identify your limits.

· **What action do I need to take to reach my goal?**
  Define your strategy.

· **When do I start taking action, and what do I have to let go?**
  Define your plan.

Again, these tasks seem very simple, but they're far from easy.

Step 2: Craft Your Life Diamond Vision and Connect With it on a Daily Basis

When you craft your vision of how you want to shine in your life from the inside out, write it down, add photos to it, and make it a habit to read it out loud every day, maybe one facet a day. You'll train your consciousness on your vision, which will influence your small daily decisions. You may think that your life is completely full, with no room in your schedule. The secret is to take one small step at a time. If you do this consequently, you'll grow exponentially. A 1% daily improvement can lead to you becoming thirty-seven times better in a year – a testament to the strength of consistency and persistence. Imagine changing 2% per day! Under glasselevator.me/5D-Leadership, you'll find more information about the eleven categories, including which actions you can take in each to evolve. Viewing the next twelve months as a long-term target, change your habits in one category for thirty days; that way, the new habit will become natural because you've changed your daily practice. Once that's done, change the next. Stack your good habits, make it easy, make change your new normal with small things like having a cold shower, creating a gratitude journal, drinking less coffee, etc. Let's now take a deeper look at the **Health** category, because this is fundamental to your being.

Your Health is Your #1 Energy Source

Look at the facets that already sparkle in your life. Maybe your career and finances. These are the ones you polished. The whole diamond won't shine overnight; it's a step-by-step process. Remember, where your focus goes, your energy flows. Health is fundamental. You need to invest energy in order to create an extraordinary life;

this can only be increased from the inside, through boosting your fitness. When you increase your energy in your body – through interval or resistance training, for example – you increase your brain's capacity and productivity, making it easier to achieve work-related goals. That's a great benefit.

Think about the advantages more energy, productivity, and happiness would bring to your life that you can achieve alone through improved fitness. For example, **how would a sexier body reflect on your love life? How would increasing your productivity impact your career, with shorter working hours or a higher salary? What would focusing on your passion look like?** Would you start painting or playing an instrument, spending more time on a bike or horseback, or walking St Jacob's Way in the Spanish countryside?

Measure Your Growth Steps

I was always sporty and regularly went to the gym twice a week, but in my early fifties I slowly but surely lost my shape and put on a few kilos. I didn't like myself in yoga classes when I held my flabby hips and my belly fat got in the way of some exercises. I know, complaining is useless. I bought a body fat scale for under thirty Euros. The first measurement result was a shock. I signed up at the nearest gym and embarked on a three-month online fitness training program. Today, I exercise every day; as a result, I like my shape again. I've lost over seven kilos, drink green smoothies for breakfast, and almost completely avoid alcohol. I walk over three kilometers a day and feel healthy and strong again. And just as I do with my health, I take care of all other facets of my life, feeling fully responsible. Now, my life just gets better and better, and I feel that I can truly influence how I feel during the day through this practice.

Embrace your life's multi-faceted brilliance with the *Life Diamond*. Explore eleven shimmering facets, each a potential wellspring of growth. Begin with a candid self-assessment, then craft your strategy to polish each area. As you embark on this journey, remember: Consistent, incremental enhancements can amplify your vibrance thirty-seven times in just a year! Prioritize your health, as it fuels all other facets. Harness today's boundless knowledge to sculpt a fitter, more energetic you and work actively to create the best version of yourself.

The Desire for Wholeness Leads to Conscious Contribution

Yes, you can have it all in life – but you **can't** increase growth in all areas at the same time. That's because you need first to consciously learn how to grow, then learn how you can maintain your current level of quality before focusing on another area. This is exactly how you created your career so far, maybe unconsciously. Some people need a second or a third marriage to learn how to lead a fulfilling love partnership. Become conscious of your status quo, taking responsibility for your growth path. A leader who lives passionately is much more inspiring than one who doesn't allow themselves to enjoy life to its fullest. In my experience, when you dedicate your life to serving the greater good, connect more deeply with your purpose and act on it daily – the quality of life improves for everyone involved. Layer by layer, you become more deeply connected; your desire to contribute grows with the happiness that you'll feel every day. Your spirituality is your connection with your source. Continue to ask yourself:

- How connected do I feel with my higher self, my trust in God, the universe, the source?

- Could my belief be stronger or deeper?

- Do I feel scarcity or abundance?

- Did I choose to feel abundance, or choose scarcity?

- Do I have a growth mindset or a scarcity mindset?

- How happy am I with my contribution, and what am I giving back to society?

- What values do I want to stand for, and be recognized for by others?

When you're committing to your growth as a 5D-Leader and learn to consciously evolve within your leadership role, you'll not only celebrate the rewards at work – you'll also evolve in all areas in life you desire. Most of all, you'll allow yourself to enjoy life to the fullest, because your contribution grows naturally when you increase your energy across all facets.

When you feel blocked in a certain area or suffer painfully, ask for specific professional advice. Maybe your health already sets a certain limit, or you're in a financially critical situation; there are solutions to escape from many crises. You may have to adapt to your environment, which can drag you down through negative energy and ingrained patterns of negative behavior. Being in an environment where friends tell you, *"You'll never make it"*, *"Don't imagine you're any better"*, or *"Do you really think you'll ever change anything about yourself?"* doesn't help. Choose better friends that inspire you and believe in your dreams. Don't be afraid of emptiness. When you grow out of your surroundings, the loneliness you can initially experience is the space you create for better friends to come into your life. I'm not excluding myself here, either. I had to let go of many that kept me down, and today I feel incredibly supported and loved. That's why it's good to find a coach, a mentor who actively supports and accompanies you on your growth path. Living a purpose-driven life will create the best version of yourself when you commit to taking full responsibility for your life, defining what you want, and acting on it daily. Do the work. How do you know that you're growing?

Your life experience will reveal it to you via a feedback cycle.

Step 3: Become Aware of the Feedback & Growth Cycle

There are two definitions of feedback, according to the *Oxford English Dictionary:*

1. Information about reactions to a product, a person's perfor- mance of a task, etc. which is used as a basis for improvement.

2. A screeching or humming sound resulting from the return of a fraction of the output signal from an amplifier, microphone, or other device to the input of the same device.

Both descriptions are right, even describing the same thing. Remember, you have an electromagnetic field around you, creating what resembles a humming or screeching sound in the field of others. Is your sound in harmony with others? If they can take your energetic wave and tune in to your frequency, you achieved a positive result. If you get negative feedback – maybe from your body, e.g. a pain or ache – or from people around you that you may not feel comfortable with, you're receiving low vibes, which means you haven't yet met your desired result. So, you can adapt and charge yourself up. You're in charge of how you react to feedback. You can enjoy it or learn from it; just don't let it pull you down. Instead, learn from what you receive by thinking or acting differently to get different results. Accept your emotions as your guides.

Experiencing Personal Growth Through Feedback

When I joined the German-based international sweets production company Storck in 2003, after ten years at P&G, I took over a team leader management role. Unfortunately, my new team rejected me at first. At Procter & Gamble, I was self-confident and successful, knowing how the game was played. But as a newbie at Storck, I became more insecure with each passing day, with my team remaining distant from me. I was lost in the beginning, as they preferred to be without me. For example, my team, consisting of nine women and one man, preferred to eat together. When they walked to the canteen daily, however, they often didn't ask me to join them. They discussed their projects and issues together, but they didn't ask me for help, since they'd worked for years together and I didn't fit in with the team at first.

I dreamed of being accepted by them, and wanted them to see me as who I really was – not the tough P&G results-oriented career woman they *seemed* to see, but the honest, compassionate, and committed team leader I wanted to be for them.

While I first couldn't change how they thought of me, I decided to change my thoughts about myself instead, remembering how appreciated I'd felt in my former roles. I visualized myself having fun with them, joining in their daily lunch meeting, becoming more deeply involved in their projects, and being their backbone during stormy times. I decided to stop thinking about why they didn't accept me; instead, I wanted to get raw and real by finding out why. I wanted to face reality and learn how I could change, so I asked my team to provide me with feedback and tell me the following three things:

1. What am I good at, what am I doing right, and should I continue doing it this way?
2. What should I start doing from now on?
3. What should I stop doing immediately?

The feedback session that followed my request was extremely hard for me. They were sitting in a circle of stools around me in the center, which felt like an official interrogation. When I asked them what I was doing right, they just answered with silence. Ten people sitting around me, silent, avoiding looking into my eyes! Whoa. I took a deep breath and asked what I *should* start doing from now on. After a pause, luckily, they started speaking. I was surprised about their wishes, ideas, and recommendations. They came up with topics like supporting them more strongly in their negotiations with other key departments, optimizing the complex order processes which were running poorly, or helping them with their order forms and Excel sheets. Nothing personal, at first. I wrote it all down; it was incredible useful information, revealing what I could do to become a better team leader for them.

Then, I asked them: *"What should I stop doing immediately?"*. Their biggest wish? I should stop interrupting them all the time while they were speaking! I was so eager to find answers for them, to be involved in their conversations, to be part of their discussions, that I simply never listened to them. Now, I'd proven that I was interested in their opinion – and this feedback session changed the game.

From the next day on, I had a new life. I was back in full leadership mode. My newfound willingness to learn from them and respect them at eye level was also my reincarnation. The team smiled when I came to the office, and I never ever again went alone to the canteen. The team opened up, asking me for individual feedback as well. They were accepting my perspectives, and we all became stronger. With the team's help, we digitized many processes and built a platform of global impact – the Storck Media Center, which is still online twenty years later, serving as a media manage-ment platform across all Storck companies and departments internationally. Working with my team and going to work was now fun, and remained a pleasure for many years.

The 4 Phases of the Feedback & Growth Circle

Phase 1: Imagine Your Goal in Life, Then Adjust Your Mindset and Actions to Meet It

Ask yourself:
Who do I want to become?
What do I want to achieve?

Now, consider: How does this higher version of you that's *already* achieved that goal act, walk, talk, look, eat, speak, and behave? How does it really feel, and how do others react to you? This exciting vision will provide you with the energy and courage to change your actions accordingly.

See the path to reach that goal stretched out in front of you.

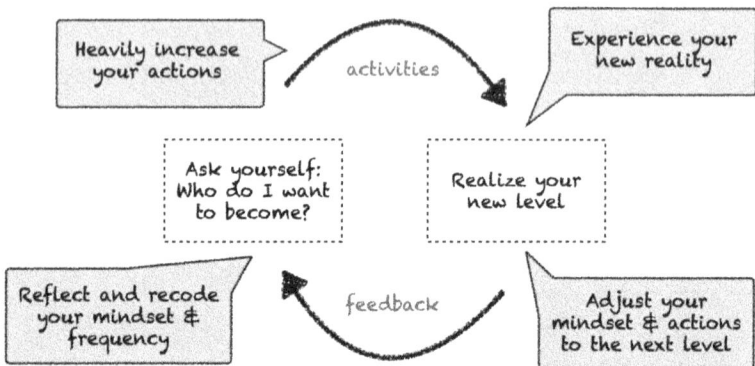

Ask your inner voice: What are the next steps to take? Learn what you need to know in order to get there, and identify the skills and steps required. Who do you need to become to reach that goal? Whom do you need to ask to learn more about your situation?

Put the information you receive through this inner reflection into action; don't be afraid. Accept the stretch, grow through your discomfort zone, and choose to believe that you're capable of becoming a better you.

Phase 2: Reflect on the Feedback and Recode Your Mindset and Frequency

You'll gain feedback from your own reality, in the form of what's happening to you. Your activities will reflect your conscious and unconscious intentions. Take this feedback, then consider what could change if you alter your mindset, including the frequency you transmit to your surroundings. Which action was right and should be increased? Every sporting champion learns through the feedback received from their trainer, as well as through the results they achieve during training or competition. See your reality as your life's playground; through daily reflection, consider what results you achieved and what led you to them. **What action did you take, and what frequency was it?**

Phase 3: Increase Your Inspired Actions

With reflection, you've identified the new actions and vibrations that led to better results. Now, *increase* these actions! When you step into the cycle, you'll receive more positive energy from the results you achieved; now, invest this energy back into your work! Allow the cycle to push you into a positive spiral, while staying open to learning from failure. (I'll explain the emotional spiral later in this chapter.) Let feedback be your guide.

In my team at Storck, I accepted feedback, reflected on it, then changed my behavior. I slowly but diligently increased my listening skills, steadily taking over more responsibility to support my team during their problematic negotiations with other departments. I supported them in their ambition to digitize complex process-es, including transferring global purchase data from programmed Excel files to SAP. We created a new project management system together, which led to increased productivity and generated a greater team spirit, as we were proud of what we could create with joint forces. This improved spirit led to better results, and so on. Your actions create a vibration; if it's positive, celebrate and consciously increase your efforts!

Phase 4: Experience Your New Reality

When you've created the reality you were dreaming of, take the time to reflect on how you achieved it. Celebrate it by thanking yourself and all your supporters – after all, your dream came true! Take a look back, to understand what caused you to get there.

Phase 5: Realize Your New Level

Become crystal-clear about what you did differently to reach this new level. What activities do you need to continue to achieve the same results? What can you do differently to gain these results even more quickly? How do you ensure these results stay stable? How could you do this with less effort?

Phase 6: Adjust Your Actions and Mindset to Maintain Your Current Level

Before you think about your next level and how your reality could be even better, make sure your great result wasn't just a one-hit wonder. Learn to stabilize your results at the highest level you dreamed of, being consciously aware of the growth you've achieved.

Advanced Cycle:
Create Your Future in Three Horizons

Imagine you go beyond your vision and create the vision behind your vision. **What's your ultimate goal, and who do you need to become to get there?** The advanced vision is to always have three goal horizons ahead of you – first, the goal you want to achieve within the coming weeks or months; second, your dream goal, which you want to achieve when the first is reached; third, your ultimate goal that's far beyond your current reality. Why is that important? Your sub-conscious mind is afraid of the unknown. When you think of a goal and aren't aware of what comes afterwards, your subconscious mind may want to protect you from this uncertainty. So, bring light to your big visions by allowing yourself to dream again.

Think of the third horizon – the incredible dream that your soul is telling you about, which still seems so far away. You may think it's too big or you don't deserve it. So, change your mind by acknowledging that it's possible. Find mentors who reached this stage.

By keeping these three goals in your broader vision, you train your subconscious mind that there's an even bigger goal to reach after the first. Through this visualization, the smaller goal suddenly becomes more possible. Your mind is flexible, so start playing with it.

Positive Emotions

Integrity

Joy

Unconditional Love

Compassion

Passion

Knowledge

Enthusiasm

Happiness

Hope

Optimism

Acceptance

Belief

Commitment

Positive Imagination

Boredom

Overwhelm

Pessimism

Sadness

Anger

Hurt

Fear

Self-pity

Guilt

Powerlessness

Doubt

Rage

Hatred

Apathy

Depression

No will to live

Negative Emotions

Step 4: The Emotional Spiral

There's one key element that keeps us from achieving what we desire. What often gets in our way are our emotions, which often interfere with our actions. We unconsciously misbehave, hurt other people through things we say or don't say, or even become unconsciously violent and ruin our relationships in the process. Let's have a look at how emotions evolve, and how we can learn to influence them.

We all experience emotions, and it's in your hands to increase the positive energy and emotions of your life through your behavior and actions. Look at the upper spiral of the illustration. Ask yourself:

· How often do I feel positive emotions during the day?

· What can I change in my life to stay in the positive zone more often?

· What do I need to start doing, and what do I need to stop doing, to feel less negative?

· What types of people or situations in my life should I let go of that constantly drag me downwards?

· How do I feel about my life?

Reflect again on your eleven *Life Diamond* facets, exploring how you want to feel in each individual area of your life. Your positive emotions rise from your imagination, head towards optimism, then expand to a higher vibrational enthusiasm. They may lead to knowing, joy, integrity, and unconditional love, the more you focus on intensifying them.

At the other end, the negative spiral starts with being overwhelmed and feeling pessimistic towards being able to change the situation you're in. So, you sink deeper into the downward spiral, feeling sadness, anger, and hurt, followed by fear, self-pity, and guilt. You lose any sense of self-worth, feeling completely powerless. You start to hate yourself and may even become enraged, resulting in depression, apathy, and maybe a complete lack of the will to live. I was there at the deepest bottom, and thought: *"There's just no way out"*.

Step 5: Escape Your Negative Emotional Spiral

You are not your emotions. You have a higher consciousness beyond them, which can help you understand the message being sent by the experience you're having. I know how it feels when you see nothing but a dark tunnel in front of you. Now, when the negative emotions want to enter my zone, I know how to turn them around and focus on the light inside of me.

EXPERIENCING EMOTIONAL TURNAROUND

I experienced heavy depression in my life, moments so dark that I couldn't find any good reason to continue. When I started out after a successful management career to become an entrepreneur, I failed so many times in my attempts to be successful that I felt like a pure failure. I did too many things at the same time for too many years and through this lack of focus in my life, there was an understandable lack of results. I was in a downward spiral. In 2019 my depression got so bad that I could hardly sleep anymore; I was obsessed with thoughts of how to bring my life to an end. Due to the loss of sleep, I could hardly concentrate during the day and my negative thoughts took over. Weirdly, I started to look for skyscrapers around me, in the hopes of finding one that was tall enough to jump from. I asked Doctor Google why I was obsessed with such thoughts and got many answers – including one telling me that a crisis in life is a fundamental part of personal growth, and mental sickness needs treatment. So I went to a psychiatrist, which was the turning point for me. My psychiatrist ordered me to go jogging every day, so I did; the jogging led to better feelings about my body, as well as about myself. On top of this, I practiced yoga every day, which helped me influence my mood. With this better mood, I gained better thoughts. From these better thoughts, I gained more energy to take action, enabling me to experience positive situations again. There's a way out of the emotional spiral, a way to change your mind and beliefs, and if you need professional help, make sure you get it. Because you're human, you can get sick, get help, and heal yourself through love. When you feel mentally healthy, combine the insight about the emotional spiral with the method you learned through exploring the *Feedback & Growth Cycle*. By taking one step after the next, it works.

Invest in your growth, accepting that you may fail on your next level with an action that worked so well for you before. Every level is different. Follow your desire, learn from your failure, adapt, and take decisive action. Be open to learning more about the theory and practice of personal growth, prioritizing learning experiences that focus on consciousness-raising topics like emotional intelligence, mindfulness, self-awareness, and unconscious bias. Seek, and you will find inspiration while becoming a better leader. Also, choose mentors that guide you on how to life your live to the fullest, blossoming in all facets. You'll find many life coaches when you search for them, like Tony Robbins, or choose to join Missy and Jon Butcher's *"Life Book"* Community – for me, the most inspiring couple who've built a multitude of incredible enterprises and who live a magical life including a deep loving relationship, a happy family life, and incredible financial wealth. Get inspired and actively build a community around you that supports your growth with love and support.

> *"One can have no smaller or greater mastery*
> *than mastery of oneself."*

— LEONARDO DA VINCI

Summary of Five Key Steps to Embark on Your Next Level

Your true growth path as a 5D-Leader starts with the desire to make all areas in your life's diamond shine. It may take a good amount of rubbing, but when you actively use the *Feedback & Growth Cycle* and learn how to accept and deal with your emotions, the level of positivity in your life will grow significantly. You'll become a happier, healthier and wholehearted 5D-Leader when you're supported by your own truth.

Step 1: Create Your Life Diamond for all eleven Categories in Your Life

Craft your vision, define your plans for how you want to experience your Health, Emotions, Love Life, Relationships, Intellect, Spirituality, Passion, Lifestyle, Career, Wealth and Contribution, then complete each task:

1. Create your vision
2. Identify your reasons
3. Identify your limits
4. Define your plan.

Step 2: Bring Your Vision to Life

Work daily with your *Life Diamond*, take action according to your plans, and become immersed in your visions.

Step 3: Use the Feedback & Growth Cycle

Check the effect of your activities. Reflect on this, recoding your mindset, frequency, and actions accordingly.

Step 4: Get Aware of Your Status Within the Emotional Spiral

Get aware of your emotions, listen and learn from your negative emotions, from any pain, and use the energy inside of you to identify intuitive action.

Step 5: Invest in Your Growth

Search for mentors and build your personal growth community.

End of Part One

By completing this first part of the book, STEPPING INTO 5D-LEADERSHIP, you've learned about the different dimensions of your reality that you can access through personal growth. You've learned methods of evolving as a purposeful 5D-Leader by dedicating your life to unlimited growth, merging your values with those of your organization, and contributing to humanity's ascension to a *Oneness Consciousness* through the positive impact you make on others through this inner and constant transformation.

Now let's move on to the second part of the book, ELEVATING 5D-LEADERSHIP CONSCIOUSNESS, which concentrates more on the impact on your team once you've internalized the lessons from the first chapters. In the following pages, you'll learn how to apply this 5D-Leadership logic to your business. I explain reasonable actions to enable a positive mindset shift in your team, inspiring your colleagues and stakeholders to increase productivity and innovation as well as intensifying collaborations. Once you experience a positive impact on your team, you'll be eager to expand it to your whole organization.

PART 2

ELEVATING 5D-LEADERSHIP CONSCIOUSNESS

TEAM TRANSFORMATION

CHAPTER 4

HUMAN-CENTERED BUSINESS TRANSFORMATION

How to take a human perspective and recode the DNA of your organization

"We believe ... in being a force for positive change in our communities."

— LEVI STRAUSS & CO

Most companies of the 19th century either evolved or disappeared. As the massive industrial firms of the past make way for hyper-connected, data-driven organizations, companies need to adapt to remain competitive. One example of a company that has successfully transformed itself into a 21st-century global data and AI leader is Levi Strauss & Co.

They claim to be a company of trailblazers and creative thinkers, committed to putting their people first. They've stuck to their aspirational values since the birth of the blue jean in 1873; throughout its long history, the company has inspired change in the marketplace, the workplace, and the world. These kinds of companies are the most successful organizations on the planet, as Richard Barrett explains in his bestseller *The Values-Driven Organization*. Consequently, understanding employees' needs and what people value is the key to creating a high-performing organization.

Mastering Digital and Cultural Transformation

Levi's demonstrates how a company which has embraced digital and cultural transformation has managed to become a data-driven innovation leader in its market, despite its long heritage. In 2020, their direct e-commerce sales increased by 52%, and their profits have grown by 14% per year over the past five years. Levi's has significantly increased its market share, demonstrating the continued strength of its brands, the versatility of its business, and the focused execution of its team's strategic plan. They also addressed their air pollution issues by committing to reducing greenhouse gas emissions, launching sustainability initiatives, and actively advocating for a more sustainable fashion industry.

Levi's puts its employees first, wants to serve a global community, is committed to a shift toward greater sustainability, and has a higher purpose than just making money. There are certainly younger companies that are much more focused on conscious business practices, such as Patagonia – but for a 19th century company, Levi's has made the transition to the 21st century with flying colors. This unprecedented ability for constant and rapid change only works if you can get your employees and leaders to constantly change and grow as well. They must understand the latest trends, along with people's deep motivations and individual needs. They must have the desire to curiously embrace the latest technologies, with the ambition and zest for constantly improving how they work together as a team.

Adapt to the Data Explosion with Higher Consciousness

Making a direct comparison between individual and organizational consciousness is difficult. However, it can be seen here that companies' consciousness can also enjoy strong vertical growth. From the 5D point of view, one could say that Levi's has managed to move into the 4D world by demonstrating a higher awareness of the planet, focusing on people and positive social change, and displaying a strong commitment to serve and support our society. They heavily invested in their employees by providing them with opportunities to learn and develop new skills, empowering them to embrace technology and drive innovation within their respective roles. One can wonder whether they'll strive to become a global 5D-company which unites people culturally and brings an even stronger contribution to social justice and the wholeness of all their employees, as well as of their suppliers from low-wage countries.

Today's Companies Have to Face an Exponentially Increasing Data Explosion

According to Statista, we have to deal with a doubling of the amount of data in the near future. In 2025, we expect a data volume of 175 zettabytes (that corresponds to data about a height of a DVD stack that goes 222 times around the earth!). In 2030, this amount is predicted to more than triple to 612 zettabytes. This exponentially growing amount must be mastered with Big Data Analytics, to filter out the golden nuggets of relevant data. At the same time, human consciousness will continue picking up speed to cope with this exponentially growing change in our world. Companies need to change faster and faster to ensure they take their people with them, transforming and inspiring them just as quickly.

To illustrate the advantages of human capacity over data (even if AI intelligence is increasing exponentially), I want you to think about your organization like it's a human organism. Imagine it has a consciousness, like humans, with the ability to sabotage itself, as well as overcoming fears and breaking through old thought patterns. To change without sacrificing its values or aspirations, the company needs to constantly recode its DNA.

The main driver of any successful business transformation is undoubtedly the strategy designed to fit the market's constantly changing requirements. But when you realize that your company exists in a 5D reality, moving between different levels of consciousness, you adopt a new perspective. You'll gain an insight into how you can develop a deeper awareness and understanding of how to become aware of and analyze this reality, then use these reflections to visualize and accelerate the transformation in your organization.

Have you ever looked at your organization from the 5D reality perspective? Do it now. What we usually do is look at our own organization from the physical perspective. When doing this, we see the buildings and structures, the hierarchy, the people, and the processes, then make a dualistic judgement about the organization's people. If we're lucky, we have a super boss; if we're unlucky, we outsmart our boss, and our daily work feels like being trapped on a treadmill. Alternatively, we may have a super boss who's supportive, but it's impossible to find true alignment with our peers.

So, from this dualistic stage, how should a transformational process in a company work?

Why Transformation Fails from a Dualistic Stage of Consciousness

To bring a practical example into our discussion about organizational transformation and consciousness, let's consider the case of a hypothetical organization, *"TechGlobal Inc."*. This is an organization that encountered significant pitfalls during its transformational journey to adapt to the data explosion. TechGlobal Inc., originally an industry leader, found itself struggling when it came to integrating advanced data analytics into its operations. Despite having access to vast amounts of data, the company faced resistance from employees who were accustomed to traditional methods of data processing and decision-making. In response, TechGlobal Inc. invested in training programs to develop new skills among its workforce, but the pace of change led to a culture clash between the new, data-driven approach and the established, intuition-based decision-making process. This discord highlighted a lack of alignment between the company's strategic goals and the employees' readiness for change.

While the company's leadership pushed for a rapid transformation, harnessing the power of big data analytics, they overlooked the necessity of bringing their people along on this journey. The Executive team, engrossed in the potential of technology, failed to lead by example in unfolding their own human potential.

They acted on the dualistic stage of consciousness, continually arguing with each other instead of searching for alignment. This oversight resulted in a workforce that felt overwhelmed rather than empowered. The transformation of TechGlobal Inc. serves as a cautionary tale. It underscores the importance of human capacity and consciousness in the face of a data explosion. The company's focus was too narrow, aiming solely at technological adoption without considering the human element – how employees interact with new technology, their fears, their resistance to change, and the need to shift mindsets alongside implementing new systems. TechGlobal Inc. learned the hard way that successful business transformation isn't just about strategy and technology; it's also about nurturing a higher consciousness within the organization. This involves developing a deeper awareness and understanding of the reality in which the company operates (encompassing a human perspective and a growth mindset), then using these insights to guide the transformation journey. It's about recognizing the organization as a living organism, with its own set of values, aspirations, and potential self-sabotaging behaviors, and leading it through growth and change with empathy and vision.

As you reflect on your own organization, it's vital to ask whether you're considering all dimensions of transformation – beyond the physical and into the realm of higher consciousness.

Are you considering the feelings, fears, and aspirations of your people as much as the raw data and technological capabilities? Are you, as a leader, embodying the change you wish to see, and are you making conscious efforts to develop not just a strategy, but also a culture that's adaptive, aware, and aligned with your transformation goals?

THE 5-DIMENSIONS PERSPECTIVE OF YOUR BUSINESS

As purposeful and conscious 5D-Leaders, we're fully aware of the company's higher purpose, the positive aspects of its culture, the significant history, and the *"higher self"* or *"future strategy"* that it wants to become and achieve. As such, we're convinced that we're on the right track with this transformational strategy. We decide to create the future.

We love and deeply embrace the diversity of the people and celebrate their individuality. We proactively support change projects internally aligned with the company's goals and ambitions. We actively shape the goals and strategies while providing constructive feedback. We feel connected to our colleagues, stakeholders, and management, and work hard to create a culture of deep mutual trust, belonging, accountability, excellence, and commitment. We regularly reflect on our results and strive for continuous internal growth that turns into tangible results. Do you agree with me, or does it sound too dreamy?

Striving to Reach Oneness in Your Organization

When we consciously try to take the 5-Dimensions perspective, we feel at one with the company and deeply connected to all the people who work in it. We also see that the organization has a positive transformative purpose, with our values complementary to the company's own. We continue to move dynamically in our positive and negative energy fields, recognizing challenges as phases of growth. In instances of open and upright cooperation, we find ways to solve blockages that have arisen. Technology and people have entered a symbiosis, helping each other to develop faster. The company has a pro-humanity vision that moves us deeply, with processes and practices in place that create a more sustainable future and even support the underprivileged through education and integration programs. We realized that money is an energy that can be better distributed; with our demand for wholeness, fulfilment, solidarity, and oneness, this energy grows faster and exponentially to serve our purpose, having a positive effect on the wellbeing of humanity.

Now, look at your current organization like a human organism, stepping back a little from logic and just reflecting:

- Which different levels of consciousness can I recognize following the examples described above?

- Do I see a strong dedication to personal growth, and do our employees believe in their impact?

- Do employees consciously work together on a high-performance level?
  Or is the company even struggling to survive on a daily basis, stuck on the 1st or 2nd dimensional level?

- What's needed to achieve a higher level?

- What kind of thought patterns does the company have in terms of its global contribution?

· What benefits and goals for humanity has the organization or company dedicated itself to?

· How did this purpose guide the company through challenges and transformations in the past?

A well-known *purpose* example here is Apple, whose founders Steve Jobs and Steve Wozniak started with the goal of developing the most user-friendly products. This commitment to innovation and design is deeply ingrained in the company's purpose, and has guided it through significant change and turbulence to achieve massive growth and a unique global impact. Apple became a leader in creating technology that's accessible to all, including people with disabilities (featuring options like VoiceOver, which helps users with visual impairments); they've also transformed how people monitor their health and fitness with the Apple Watch. In terms of their environmental initiatives, they're committed to becoming carbon-neutral by 2030. A great purpose is a driver for growth. However small your company is, assign to it a massive transformational purpose serving a human need; choose to engage in a company that wants to transform into a conscious business. If you want to go deeper into the topic of exponentially growing companies with impressive purpose-driven examples, I recommend reading the 2nd edition of the mind-blowing book *Exponential Organizations 2.0* by Peter Diamandis and Salim Ismail, based on profound analysis.

The Soul and Heartbeat of an Organization

What about the *soul* of your company? What does it touch deep inside you? How does it stimulate the culture, goals, and overall ambition of your organization? What does your company do for the environment and humanity? What positive and lasting impact does it seek to make? What UN Sustainable Development Goals is it committed to – and do you see these as authentically connected to the company's values, or just window-dressing and greenwashing?

Now, imagine the *heartbeat* of your organization. Which rhythms and cycles of business operations are central to the company – in other words, what keeps it alive? Does it pump regularly, or does it suffer cardiac arrhythmia or even cardiac arrest?

Here, Amazon and its focus on customer-centricity illustrates the cardio fitness analogy well. Features like customer reviews, the Prime service, and one-click ordering could be considered the company's *"heartbeat"* – the consistent, ongoing processes keeping it alive and thriving. What are those in your company, especially in the area you're responsible for? Where does your company's heart beat unimpeded, and where are there constrictions in the flow? How can its heart beat better, lighter, and more consistently? Which cycle must it form to do so, and which stations must be considered? How does the company react to increased stress? How quickly does it calm its heartbeat again after exceptional stress? In your opinion, how fit is it for heavy loads? Adopting this human perspective at your company helps you to gain a holistic overview, as well as new insights that push your problem-solving ahead.

The Innovation-Blocking Power of the Immune System

Let's go further with this human view of your organization. If you can see the purpose, soul, and heartbeat of your organization and are able to describe it vividly, you create ideas and visualizations that will help you drive transformation and change.

It starts with your imagination and connecting yourself with your company in an authentic and truthful way.

Now think about the *immune system* of your company. It has an indescribable, unconscious power to protect the business from new ideas and ways of thinking. What are the fifty reasons why your company should not change? What main reasons are usually given for attacking innovation? Do you often hear sentences like: *"We can't do it, since no-one's ever done it before"*, or *"It's too radical for us to change"*, or *"Only small (or big) companies can change in this way"*, or *"This is beyond my responsibility"*, or *"The customers won't buy it"*? Do these statements lack any supportive data, and are they just posing as wisdom from experience? The experts in your organization prefer to explain to you how it can't be done. The reason is simple: The day before something is a breakthrough, it's a crazy idea. Understand, see, and feel the immune system of your company, visualizing how brave, disruptive ideas have been attacked in order to kill them off. On the other hand, you should also think about the benefits of your immune system. What incredible healing powers does it possess, even when it's been attacked by foreign invaders? How well does it work when a risk has been taken and something has gone wrong?

The immune system is a big challenge, especially for traditional and hierarchical organizations, because its focus on efficiency, process, and bureaucracy massively opposes innovation. In my work with leading companies, reducing bureaucracy and moving towards a more humane organization are everyday challenges which I could write ten more books about. Fortunately, someone has already published a masterpiece about this topic. For those who want to delve deeper into the subject, I recommend Gary Hamel and Michelle Zanini's outstanding *Humanocracy: Creating Organizations as Amazing as the People Inside Them.* It even offers an online evaluation of your company's status with the Bureaucratic Mass Index (BMI) survey. (You'll find the link in the *Sources* section of this book.)

Answering the questions about your company's purpose, soul, heartbeat, and immune system and bringing it into perspective with the highest state of consciousness – oneness – will shed light on the dimensions of reality your company is acting within today.

Five Steps to Take a Human Perspective and Recode Your Company's DNA

Operating with a higher consciousness is a metaphor for deep cultural and operational change. It's about changing the ways a company operates, makes decisions, and interacts with its stakeholders. This process often requires a shift in mindset at all levels of the organization, new leadership styles, and innovative approaches. With the next steps, I demonstrate a new approach – however, these aren't simply a description of a new change management model. Taking a *human* perspective will help you get connected with your team and organization on a deeper level. It's an invitation to reflect on your company's purpose and its capacity to adapt and to evolve, similar to the biological concepts of mutations and constant evolution.

Step 1: Take a Human Perspective on Your Organization
Write down and consider:

· What is the purpose of my company?

- What is ingrained in our code and destiny?
  Is it innovation, productivity, ... ?

- What is the dormant potential of the purpose that needs to be awakened?

- What is our company's soul?

- What makes its heart beat? What are its rhythms?

- Where does the company come from? What is its heritage?

- How does it want to appear in future?
  How will it transform to get there?

- Which old behaviors, thought patterns, practices, and habits can we let go of that no longer align with the company's aspirations?

Phrase it in your own words first, considering how you can align your thoughts with your company's vision. Then, share these insights and perspectives with your team and your peers – or better still, do the task together right from the start. You can set up a workshop, use a classical SWOT analysis, conduct cultural audits, or set up a brainstorming session to work on the vision. Remember to ask your team for their own view. This will help you identify the transformation's goals and objectives beyond the company's "normal" vision and goals. To shed light on your reality, you want your organization to operate with a higher consciousness.

Yes, it takes courage to connect and think this way – first with your team, then with the broader organization. Follow your inner voice. Your company's a living being, not a physical three-dimensional construct as many understand it. It's been created by people, after all.

Step 2: Analyze the Blocks and Distortions Influencing the Energy Flow

Imagine that when you're linked with the energy of your organization and visualize the cycles and processes (e.g. the heartbeat as described above), you may see many blocks and distortions stopping the flow. Link the information you receive with your current feedback systems, like internal audits or employee surveys. When you become aware of these blocks and distortions from multiple dimensions, and understand the negative internal or external interferences disturbing the communication transfer and the processes, bring them all together – then imagine you have the power to pull them out and clean the energy flows!

What? Yes, get rid of them, push them out, release them. Imagine this cleaning process continuing from the moment you first imagined it, telling others what you want to get rid of and release. Believe it or not, what you can hold in your head, you can hold in your hand. (This is a mind exercise to help you believe in your power and impact.) If you can imagine a possible solution, your intuition will spark ideas on how to do it step by step, getting closer to your company's ideal future self in the process. No matter how small your impact, you can find solutions for many inner problems if you create space to invite your intuition in. Before we create the action plan for transformation, we need to do a deep dive into the analysis.

Step 3: Increase Resilience and Become Aware of Self-Sabotaging Patterns

Organizations are run by people, and our subconscious minds permanently run thought patterns that stop us from moving on. When you learn to recognize your own self-sabotaging patterns, then catch and release them, you can teach others to help themselves in a similar situation. Many companies have already introduced resilience-building programs, mindfulness training, or coaching sessions designed to address and remedy self-sabotage. As resilience needs to be built up, it requires practice – by helping others identify their patterns, we grow faster together. Some of the most common self-sabotage patterns people face are:

· Overload
   When you're challenged with overload, take a step back from your work. Pause, then become aware of your breathing. Write down all the things in your head, until nothing more comes to mind. Prioritize and make decisions. Listen to yourself, align your query with your future self. Relax. In their working lives, some people are forced to manage endless queues of people, all waiting for service. There's no way forward except completing one step after the next, never forgetting to take a physical break from time to time given how long the queue is. As managers and leaders, we're more likely to face mental than physical overload, and there's only one technique that works – to focus on breathing and identifying the most important task, then going on.

- **Options Overflow**
Another pattern is having too many options. We see this again and again in our consultancy projects, where people are afraid to focus. If this happens, at least try to find your center. Listen carefully to each option. (Individually or as a team.) Collect and gather facts about the options. Combine data with intuition; most importantly, understand that contemplating too many options represents a self-sabotaging pattern which thwarts your concentrated action to achieve transformative change. If you reflect on the purpose, soul, and heartbeat of your company, what really matters?

- **Quitting**
An often-used self-sabotage pattern is quitting, where people stop in the middle of the process because they prefer to stay in their comfort zone. If you don't accept that you sometimes must find your way through difficulties, you'll never reach magical results. How many project ideas have been elaborated and simply never brought to life, because ...? Finishing comes before perfection.

- **Time Management Issues**
Time is limited, so not valuing your time will always lead to stress or burnout. Because your subconscious is telling you, *"Hey, you had the time – but you spent it on less important tasks!"*, procrastination causes tremendous stress. Be aware that this is a thought pattern. Write a time-script of your day from getting up in the morning until late evening. By doing this, either manually or through

the support of AI, you'll see how you spent your time. Share this breakdown with your team, then ask them what they do during their regular working week. Even though they won't appreciate this task in the beginning, remind them that awareness is a core requirement for transformation. When the results are in, analyze them, then relay them back to the whole team. Being productive is fun; great time management is uncomfortable but makes you happy in the long run.

· **Overplanning**
This is another tough one, as many companies insist on having a full plan for everything. Yes, you need a plan, and you need to stick to it. However, there's a tendency to over-plan tasks, especially when people try to control the outcome. Determine whether you identify a self-sabotaging thought pattern when you don't reach a goal; stepping back from your over-planned task lists before expecting to achieve another outcome can help.

Resilience requires awareness. Discuss the importance of resilience with your team, including how it relates to vertical development. Share self-sabotaging thought patterns with them, then explore strategies for building resilience, managing adversity, and overcoming fear. Let them become aware of the connection between embracing the unknown and fostering innovation. When you overcome your fears of talking about these human perspectives in your team, you'll change the game.

Step 4: Imagine Your Organization as the Ideal

Take the time for an awareness practice. Imagine closing your eyes and embodying your company's sole mission – in other words, its reason for being on the planet. Connect with the soul of your company, linking its heart with your own. Imagine it's a diamond inside, glowing with the positive energy people exude when they collaborate and create something new. Fall in love with the people around you. They all share the same light inside. You're all connected, wishing to realize the best version of yourselves. Feel the bright light, then look at the purpose of your company. What is the change you want to create in the world? Then look at the DNA strands of your organization. What are its ingrained fundamentals, and which parts need renewal? What will the future version of the company achieve, produce, and create? What will it support and accelerate? To achieve this faster, what should it start doing now? And what should it stop doing immediately? What kind of recoding is needed to achieve the next version?

To see the bright future, imagine your company evolving into a new market. To do this, how does its purpose need to come alive? What are the next steps? With whom do you have to connect to discuss and develop the ideas you've just visualized? You don't have to be the CEO of a company to think that big; just be a 5D-Leader at heart. To practice this, you can find a guided 5D-Business activation at glasselevator.me/5D-Leadership.

Step 5: Create an Action Plan
by Transforming Your Realizations

- Write down everything that came up in your reflections from Step 1 to 4. You've gained significant insight into your company's purpose, soul, heartbeat, and immune system, remaining aware of typical self-sabotaging patterns.

· Sketch out an action plan for yourself, trusting your intuitions. What blocks innovation in your company – the human mind, or the lack of technology? Be raw and real with your analysis. Now, bring it into alignment with your level of impact. What can you do to accelerate change?

· Involve your team by sharing your ideas and reflections with them. Let them analyze the situation with the same systematic approach you used to create your ideas.

· Connect your analysis with the data you need to prove your findings. If there's no data available, ask colleagues and experts for their perspective. Bring your ideas into alignment with the company's goals, strategies, and vision. If your ideal vision of the company goes beyond the current one, then congratulations – you're maybe thinking bigger than your own management! Find allies to support you. When following your intuition and ideas, you may experience serendipity, an unplanned fortunate discovery. (For example, you might meet the person who's best able to support you at that moment.) It's not just about following your crazy ideas, but also about finding ways to strengthen your intuition while improving the company's outcomes.

· Prioritize actions, set realistic milestones, and find accurate ways to measure progress. (You can use common project management tools and techniques to aid with the implementation.) Involve stakeholders by letting them reflect on your thoughts. Accept that not all your ambitions will come to life.

"An organization cannot evolve beyond its leadership's stage of development."

— FRÉDÉRIC LALOUX,

Author of *Reinventing Organizations* and New Work Thought Leader

You may feel first alone and irritated with this unusual path for transformation, telling yourself: "This is for others. It's not me who can do it. This has no logic – I'm just a very, very small light in this huge organization with no impact at all ...!" If that's the case, please go back to Part One of the book and ignite your 5D-Leadership awareness! Playing with these new perspectives leads to new insights, creative ideas, and (with action) new results.

Summary of the 5 Key Steps to Drive Transformation

Embody the change you wish to see and inspire alongside your team. Any business needs to adapt to rapid change while maintaining a focus on human values and consciousness. Levi Strauss & Co are beacons of such an evolution. They've demonstrated that longstanding companies can indeed pivot into data-driven and AI-enhanced entities without losing sight of their core values, acutely managing the shift from a traditional to a digital and culturally inclusive business model. Maintaining values is important amidst technological and market change; this integrity is required to navigate the data explosion without ever losing sight of the role of human insight. To understand your place in an interconnected world beyond mere profit, view your company through the 5-Dimensional lens of consciousness. This allows you to identify and overcome internal resistance hindering innovation and growth. Companies which openly adapt to exponentially expanding technologies, operate with a devotion to higher consciousness, and dedicate themselves to employee empowerment, sustainability, and societal contribution will thrive.

Step 1: Take a Human Perspective on Your Organization

Discover the soul of your company by reflecting on its purpose, heritage, and future aspirations. Engage your team in meaningful dialogue to align your company's vision with its deeper human elements.

Step 2: Analyze the Blocks and Distortions Influencing the Energy Flow

Visualize and confront the blocks that hinder your organization's energy flow. Use a healing mindset to 'cleanse' these barriers and open up new channels for innovation and communication.

Step 3: Increase Resilience and Become Aware of Self-Sabotaging Patterns

Recognize and dismantle self-defeating behaviors within your company. Implement resilience-building practices to foster a supportive culture that overcomes fear and embraces growth.

Step 4: Imagine Your Organization as Ideal

Picture the ideal future of your company. Connect with its core mission and imagine the necessary changes in its DNA to manifest this reality. Involve your team to share and cultivate this vision. Listen to the 5D-Business activation at glasselevator.me/5D-Leadership.

Step 5: Share Your Thoughts and Experiences With Your Team

Translate your insights and visualizations into a concrete action plan. Encourage collective brainstorming, validate ideas with data, and prioritize actions to align with the company's larger goals and strategies.

Armed with this newly gained human perspective and a deeper understanding of the different levels of consciousness within your business, let's now dig deeper into the true human nature. To do this, we'll discover how to improve performance through nurturing a diverse culture of excellence.

CHAPTER 5

NURTURING A DIVERSE CULTURE OF EXCELLENCE

Balancing energies to drive creativity, innovation, and performance

*"The business of business
is improving the state of the world."*

— MARC BENIOFF,
Co-Founder, Chairman and CEO of Salesforce

I f you want to prevail against your competitors, you need to encourage your team to perform at their best. In the past, many companies have fueled this drive via aggressively encouraging employees to unleash their forces against *"enemy"* companies. Unfortunately, embracing an aggressive mindset by *"bashing the competitor"* leads to competitiveness that's not only directed externally, but also between each of the company's teams.

Fortunately, in today's world, a hostile statement of intent like Nike's 1990s *"Crush Adidas"* slogan has gone out of style. Today, Nike's vision and mission is "To bring inspiration and innovation to every athlete in the world. This mission drives us to do everything we can to expand human potential". *And they add:* "If you have a body, you are an athlete". What a development! This statement includes male and female energies; Nike had to learn if they don't focus on Yoga, other brands like *Lululemon* will show up to master this sporting area. Diversity, inclusion, and even non-competitive sports are now fully integrated into Nike's vision. Any spark of aggression or dominance has gone, yet they still manage to promote performance.

This is a worthwhile vertical evolution for a statement of purpose in favor of humanity. Expanding human potential also raises the issue of male and female energies. When both work together eye-to-eye, co-creation, collaboration, and mutual support amplify resilience and the ability to make compromises. This allows symbioses and promotes trust in one's own intentions, which in turn promotes creativity. Numerous scientific researchers state that diverse and inclusive teams are the engines of innovation (e.g. *Great Place to Work* insights). Balancing female and male energies is healthy, because we're all connected through energy fields. Although we all have both energies inside us, one side is more dominant in our physical expression. Consequently, we can support each other to grow and evolve. My career was often supported by men, with my bosses providing me with the safety I needed to rise and shine each day. They also evolved through the inspiration and energies they received from the women in the organization. I had to learn to increase my masculine energies to be capable of winning in business, but also learned that I can only awaken my full potential after bringing myself into energetic balance.

"Inclusivity means not just 'We're allowed to be there', but we are valued. I've always said: smart teams do amazing things, but truly diverse teams will do impossible things."

— CLAUDIA BRIND-WOODY,

BM Managing Director

Claudia Brind-Woody is a prominent figure in the business world, best known for her work at IBM. In addition to her significant contributions to the tech industry, she is widely recognized for her advocacy of diversity and inclusion, particularly within the LGBTQ+ community. She is committed to creating a more equitable and inclusive world, both in the corporate environment and in society at large. She shared her powerful message in a poem that you'll find in the book's online resources section: **glasselevator.me/5D-Leadership**

Discovering and fully developing the masculine and feminine forces and emotions within you and your team will allow you to make the greatest contribution. You'll achieve excellence in your diverse team with the knowledge of how to activate both energies.

In this chapter, you'll learn how to discover and fully develop the masculine and feminine forces and emotions within yourself. This experience will allow you to inspire your team to achieve greater contributions, more productive collaborations, and stronger resilience, while providing even more space to grow.

BALANCING DIVERSE ENERGIES IN BUSINESS

Salesforce has been a pioneer in integrating the values of equality, trust, and customer success into its core business strategy, demonstrating the fusion of assertive, forward-driving masculine energy with inclusive, nurturing feminine energy. Under the leadership of co-CEOs Marc Benioff and Keith Block, they implemented the 1-1-1 model of philanthropy. This model commits the company to giving 1% of its product, 1% of its equity, and 1% of its employees' time back to the community, integrating the traditionally masculine drive for growth and success with a nurturing commitment to societal welfare and community support. The company's approach to leadership also emphasizes emotional intelligence and mindfulness, integrating spaces for meditation on every floor of their office buildings, harmonizing the goal-oriented drive with self-awareness and care for employees' wellbeing. The coalescence of masculine and feminine energies has woven a tapestry of corporate innovation and compassionate capitalism under Benioff's and Block's stewardship. The company's 1-1-1 philanthropic model stands as a testament to the harmonious blend of market conquest with community nurture, catapulting Salesforce not just to the zenith of its industry but also to the vanguard of social change. Here, the vigor of ambition meets the virtue of altruism, creating an enterprise that pulsates with the energy of achievement and the warmth of generosity.

Salesforce thrives commercially while advancing societal wellbeing, embodying the balance of energies across the spectrum of its operation while embracing an inclusive performance culture.

This is a great example of how balanced energies empower business – but how can we activate them within you and ignite them in your team?

MY JOURNEY TO ENERGETIC BALANCE

During my time at Sony, especially in the last three years as Operations Head and member of the Executive team, I was surrounded by men almost from morning to night. I had many female employees, but my peers and my superiors, with whom I spent most of the time in meetings during the days, were all male. Every woman who's been in a similar position knows how exhausting that is, because you simply feel unbalanced over time. In the beginning, I wanted to be exemplary and was proud to be the first women in the history of this company that pushed through this glass ceiling. This had its price, but the fact that I was seeking to recover my inner balance was also my good luck. Through a colleague, I'd rediscovered horse riding, which reminded me of my girlhood. This made my inner child happy on a regular basis, as I started to spend a lot of time with horses – first at weekends, then when I started going on horse-riding vacations. That was my energetic balance. At the weekends, I was out and about with a group of leisure horse riders in the idyllic countryside of Brandenburg, feeling alive and unburdening my brain, being in nature, in a healing world as we galloped through the woods and across the fields, or rode in a leisurely manner through flower meadows. Then I started to book exciting vacations on horseback, including cantering along the beaches of Portugal on

Lusitanos, and riding through the desert of Jordan on Arabian thoroughbreds. On another holiday I went to Kenya, rode through the fascinating landscape of the Chyulu Hills, had a race with a gentle giraffe, and encountered elephants, gazelles, and big cats. These adventurous safaris loaded up my batteries for the times back in the office.

Then a twist of fate helped me on my way. Our CEO at Sony, who'd brought me to the company, was leaving. The European management announced further restructuring and I took the opportunity to finish my assignment as well. A generous termination agreement was my parting gift. I was determined to open a new chapter and deepen mine inwards. Reading the book *Zen Mind, Zen Horse – The Science and Spirituality of Working with Horses* written by Dan Hamilton, a Harvard-trained brain surgeon who's also a horse trainer, I was fascinated by the effect working with horses can have on the brain, especially the right hemisphere. That was exactly what I needed; I felt my left brain was overworked, and was seeking to experience the evolution first-hand. Therefore, right after leaving Sony, I went in search of a teacher who matched my longing and found him immediately – a spiritual riding master who teaches riding in balance, the Portuguese and world-renowned horse master Manuel Jorge de Oliveira. I decided to buy a Lusitano stallion from him and became his student for the subsequent five years, an experience that's shaped my life very deeply to this day. What did I learn about excellence, lightness, and the balance of energy?

"The only way to live your live is to give your best every single second of your life."

— MANUEL JORGE DE OLIVEIRA

Manuel's a living legend, known for his high-class teachings in classical riding and his unique approach to horsemanship. His philosophy emphasizes the mental, emotional, and physical balance between the horse and rider.

He stresses the importance of achieving harmony and unity between rider and horse. This unity is essential for maintaining balance, as it allows both to move as one entity. The rider's ability to align their movements with the horse's natural motions is crucial. A significant focus is placed on the rider's posture and seat, as these are fundamental to maintaining balance on horseback. I was taught to sit upright and centered, with a relaxed but alert posture that follows the horse's movements without causing disturbance.

Manuel taught me to listen first and become aware of the horse's needs and signals. He advocates for lightness in the rider's touch. This approach helps in maintaining balance by ensuring that the horse isn't overburdened or confused by heavy-handed commands. Balance isn't only physical, but also involves the mental and emotional states of horse and rider. It's also the basis for developing a trusting and deep relationship; to respect the horse's pace of learning, sometimes you have to wait for the horse. Patience is needed when you want to grow together, as grass doesn't grow faster when you pull on it.

Daily progress is the key to learning, not speed.

What I loved most was the philosophical perspective of the "vertical" riding theory. Manuel's perspective emphasizes the beauty and depth of connection achievable through disciplined practice and mutual respect to create a balanced, harmonious relationship where both horse and rider are comfortable, confident, and capable of performing at their best.

In 2015 I visited Manuel at his Quinta in Portugal, found my dream horse Fuego at his stable, a four-year-old grey Lusitano with a magnificent black mane. Manuel invited me to teach me and join him on his farm during the year. I felt like I was in heaven and spent weeks riding in Portugal that year. The atmosphere in the Quinta was unique; the discipline of the professional riders fascinated me to the bone. There was silence and concentration, but also lightness and joy in the serious and intensive work with the horses. Being one with the horse is the foundation of "vertical" riding training. The oneness with God, with the universe, with oneself and as a rider in the connection with the horse, but also with the space in which one moves, with any spectators, with all the energy that's in us and also around us – simply everything. Manuel taught me to acknowledge the key difference between the divine female and masculine energies and that we need to embrace both in us and be aware of their differences to reach inner and outer harmony in life.

For those who want to learn more about this magnificent master, read the book *A Breath of Eternity*, his memoir and philosophical exploration of his lifelong connection with horses and his journey to find inner calm and peace.

THE MASCULINE AND FEMININE ENERGIES

We're all spiritual beings having a human experience. Diversity starts in our minds. When we expand the understanding of ourselves and gain a holistic understanding of our feminine and masculine forces alike and embrace the interconnection of universal opposites, we foster a more balanced and integrated approach to personal and professional challenges. This holistic perspective allows us to navigate complexities with greater wisdom and creativity, ultimately leading to a more fulfilling and harmonious life. We ignite our full energetic capacity. How do these different energies affect our business?

Masculine energies are associated with a demanding leadership style, while feminine energies are associated with sensuality,

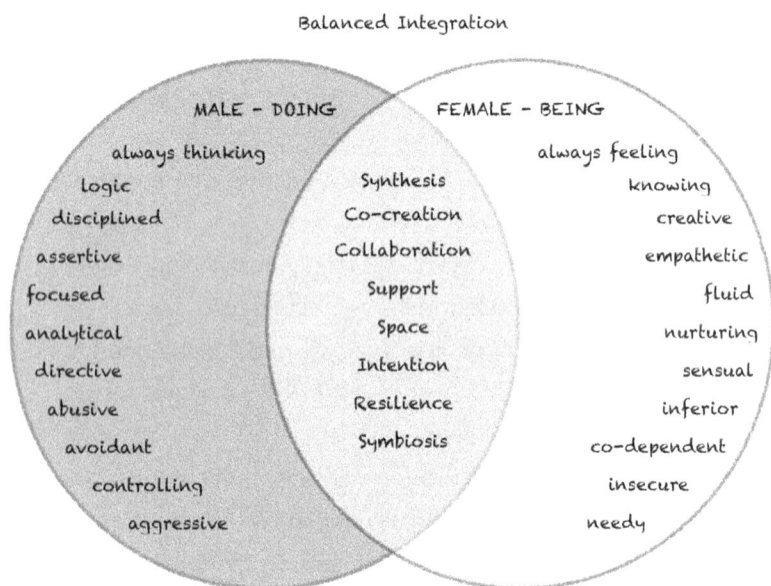

Balanced Integration

MALE – DOING   FEMALE – BEING

MALE – DOING		FEMALE – BEING
always thinking	Synthesis	always feeling
logic	Co-creation	knowing
disciplined	Collaboration	creative
assertive	Support	empathetic
focused	Space	fluid
analytical	Intention	nurturing
directive	Resilience	sensual
abusive	Symbiosis	inferior
avoidant		co-dependent
controlling		insecure
aggressive		needy

collaboration, movement, and nurture. When you want to create a sense of respect and transformation in a team, you need to balance both energies; this helps create a team that leads with creativity, harmony, and wellness. The masculine energies promote targets and getting things done individually, while the feminine allow collaboration and getting things done together. We live in a world where the masculine, *"always thinking"* mind, powered by controlling, aggressive, focused, and analytical energies, is too dominant, while the feminine, *"always feeling"* mind, powered by creative, knowing, empathetic, fluid, and nurturing energies, is suppressed. Naturally, this suppression leads, often subconsciously, to the victimization and co-dependency of women. If we create a balance of these energies within us, we receive more co-creation, collaboration, synthesis, and intentional actions and decisions. Worth giving it a try?

Step 1: Harmonizing Dual Energies for Team Synergy

1. Create awareness in yourself regarding your current mental model of masculine and feminine energy. Each of us sees the world through a certain filter. This filter, our mental model, is made up of our judgments, assumptions, and life experiences with all kinds of individuals. If you can identify your mental models, you'll become more open-minded and learn how to question your thinking. Both masculine and feminine energies are essential, as everyone has both energies within them. It's crucial to find a balance between both energies to create positive change. Invite your team members to become aware of their different energies as well. You can find a guided activation to celebrate your masculine and feminine energies at glasselevator.me/5D-Leadership

2.   Discuss in your team how the energies are currently balanced.

- What's dominant and what's suppressed?
- Where do we need feminine energy?
- Where do we need masculine energy?
- How do we recognize those qualities within us?
- What would be different if we allowed more balance?
- Given we're not always displaying our best energy, how can we improve our strength and resilience?
- How do masculine and feminine energies influence us on a mental, spiritual, physical, and energetic level?
- What's different, and how does this affect us in complex projects?

Step 2: Conscious Integration for Organizational Health

Encourage your team to be self-aware and pay attention to the here and now; talk about the different energies and their strengths when they come together. By being aware of how both masculine and feminine energies function, one can achieve a balance. Discuss how the masculine and feminine perspective relates to your organization.

1.   Taking the male perspective, review the areas of your responsibility within a holistic male view (*"systems thinking"*).
2.   Now take the feminine perspective (*"relational thinking"*). What's different? How does it feel different?

Discuss the differences you see from a holistic perspective, bringing them together to achieve an *"organism thinking"*.

What do you recognize? What do you learn from the less dominant energy? What behaviors are related to each side, and what's the resulting synthesis?

Step 3: Vulnerability as a Leadership Strength

Encourage your team to model vulnerability. Admitting you were wrong or needed help shows that vulnerability doesn't equate to weakness. By showing your team that vulnerability is OK, you encourage them to be more open and honest with each other, which can lead to better communication and collaboration. Brené Brown's famous TED Talk on *The Power of Vulnerability* has over 62 million views for a reason. Leaders should reward vulnerability and risk-taking, showing team members that these traits are not only accepted but *valued*. In this way, they encourage open communication and the free exchange of ideas, creating a climate of trust and creativity.

Step 4: Excellence Through Personal Mastery

Promote personal mastery among your colleagues and employees. Mastery means always giving your best, while working this way allows you to feel a deep sense of accomplishment. We all have good days and bad days, and doing our best sometimes leads to great results, sometimes to mediocre ones. While this is perfectly normal, it's crucial to become aware of why your performance was weak. Today, there are also many ways to measure one's internal performance levels, such as the *Oura* Ring, which measures sleep habits and quality, activity levels, heartrate and resting pulse, and oxygen levels, providing transparency into the impact of lifestyle habits on one's performance. Excellence encourages personal growth and improvement – and it's the *process*, not just the outcome, that's valued.

Conscious people strive for personal excellence because they know the importance of personal growth and improvement, not only to achieve their self-set goals but more importantly to achieve their full potential. Achievement and giving your best also always mean allowing yourself enough time for rest and recreation.

We need to shift from aggressive, competitive business tactics to a balanced, inclusive approach that harnesses both masculine and feminine energies for creativity, innovation and performance. This starts with moving away from rivalry towards fostering collaboration and mutual growth – a shift which starts with your own energetic balance. As a conscious 5D-Leader, you encourage the development of both your masculine and feminine energies while striving to evolve these in your team, using diversity as a core strength.

> *"Let excellence be your brand ... When you are excellent, you become unforgettable. Doing the right thing, even when nobody knows you're doing the right thing, will always bring the right things to you."*
>
> — OPRAH WINFREY

Summary of Four Key Steps to Nurture a Diverse Culture of Excellence:

Step 1: Harmonizing Dual Energies for Team Synergy

Cultivate team awareness of both masculine and feminine energies, encouraging an open-minded approach to balance these forces. Explore how integrating these energies can improve resilience and performance in complex projects. Check out the guided activation to celebrate your masculine and feminine energies at glasselevator.me/5D-Leadership.

Step 2: Conscious Integration for Organizational Health

Foster self-awareness within your team regarding the balanced integration of masculine and feminine energies. Engage in discussions that blend these perspectives for a holistic "organism thinking" that benefits the organization.

Step 3: Vulnerability as a Leadership Strength

Model vulnerability to show that it's a sign of courage, not weakness. Encourage open, honest communication, and demonstrate that vulnerability can foster trust, creativity, and innovation.

Step 4: Excellence through Personal Mastery

Promote personal mastery as a path to excellence. Emphasize the importance of giving one's best, leveraging tools to measure performance, and recognizing the significance of balance, including rest and recreation, in achieving personal growth.

Now you realize the power of male and female energies, how to activate them in your team by increasing the awareness of their differences and their positive effects when they act in balance. Let's dive deeper into how to help your team to further grow vertically and raise the team spirits to the highest level.

Chapter 6

ELEVATING EXTRAORDINARY TEAM SPIRIT

Your employees' personal growth is as important as your company's growth

"Customers will never love your company until your employees love it first."

— SIMON SINEK

A ccording to *Forbes Business*, companies that have a program in place to engage their employees enjoy 233% more customer loyalty than those that don't. In addition, according to the research, employers could have prevented 78% of the reasons employees had for quitting if they'd taken care of their people by connecting them with their needs.

A major cause of employee disruption is a lack of *Wertschätzung* (appreciation). Many companies have understood that elevating their customers' journey is crucial to increasing their loyalty, and the same is true of their employees. Higher employee engagement translates to a better customer experience, higher customer satisfaction, and higher revenues for their organization. But even when engaged leaders are committed to elevating the employee experience, they often find themselves too limited to influence the many factors at play. Depending on the size of your organization, you may have little influence on the public image of the employer or its recruiting process. But other areas – like your team's integration efforts, your employees' development, and the ongoing process of building loyalty to your company – are areas of direct impact.

In this chapter, you'll learn how to create a positive, deeply touching experience for your team with the 6 *Magic Questions*, helping them grow beyond their business role. I'll also offer you tools to assess your Team Spirit Level as a starting point to foster trust, authenticity, and collaboration while increasing overall accountability.

"Take care of your employees and they'll take care of your business."

— SIR RICHARD BRANSON

BECOME THE DRIVING FORCE FOR PERSONAL GROWTH IN YOUR ORGANIZATION

Seeing the employee experience and its many touchpoints, which are highly individual, is essential to gain a holistic picture. When examined in depth, this offers many opportunities for improvement and positive transformation, which I'll discuss further in the third part of the book. During this chapter, I'll concentrate on development and personal growth, including the methods and tools supporting you as a leader to increase your team's awareness, while fostering collaboration by boosting happiness and engagement levels. Helping others to increase their sense of self-worth is a leadership style that fires up love for your company!

If the topic of employee experience and how to improve the overall happiness in your company appeals to you, I'd like to recommend Tony Hsieh's *Delivering Happiness: A Path to Profits, Passion, and Purpose*, a wonderful guide which brings a competitive advantage to valuing employees. When (for example) Tony's company Zappos focused on employee happiness, it led to a significantly improved customer experience and increased profits. Among the book's many valuable tips and stunning insights, you'll learn that Zappos offered employees a $2,000 bonus to quit if they weren't happy, which ultimately led to a more engaged and motivated workforce! Crazy ideas can lead to great profit.

Personal growth offers an enormous field for limitless learning, because every step of development contributes to the individual's quality of life. People want to be significant and live their life to the fullest on their own terms. Lead without authority. Hierarchy is naturally accepted through earned respect, rather than through an impressive title.

In past decades, mastery was focused only on people's skill levels and capacity to increase profit. It's true that new skills and capabilities make people more valuable to a company and increase their personal marketability and career potential. But the next generations demand more from life than career and profit alone; they also want wholeness, to live on a healthy planet, and to have a positive vision for the future. These goals seem currently out of reach. Since there's no planet B, be the change.

For our inner system to thrive, we need to stop the war being fought inside of us. 5D-Leaders who support the rise of humanity commit to oneness practice every day. True masters of their life deserve respect due to the positive development that's occurred inside of them. When you've reached pure integrity and authenticity, that's visible for many people around you; however, it won't free you from opponents inhabiting lower dimensions, who are still in the process of realizing their reality. When you can create a lasting, positive experience for those around you through your words and actions, combined with the flowing spirit you're able to inspire, you're a great asset to any company. Your capacity to enforce collaboration, loyalty, resilience, and innovation are priceless. You'll naturally increase your team's ability to adapt and create, learn faster, optimize health, and most of all, raise people's happiness. This is possible because you live by your own rules, dedicating yourself to growth. The more you invest in your personal learning journey, the better you'll be able to help others grow beyond their expectations. The vast personal development opportunities aren't yet fully exploited, so there's huge potential here to increase employee retention.

Fostering a Culture of Continuous Development

A great example of ongoing dialogue and the *Wertschätzung* (appreciation) derived from good work shifting performance and driving better results is Adobe's transition to effective performance management. Adobe found that their annual performance reviews were not only a drain on time, but also negatively affected employee engagement and retention. They decided to overhaul their review system to promote ongoing dialogue and development, which aligns with the themes of personal growth and team spirit.

In 2012, Adobe replaced its annual performance review process with the *"Check-In"* framework. This system emphasizes regular, real-time feedback between managers and employees, without ratings or rankings. It focuses on setting clear expectations, providing ongoing feedback and development, and recognizing good work throughout the year.

The outcomes: Adobe saw a 30% reduction in voluntary turnover. Managers reported that their teams were more likely to meet or exceed expectations after the shift, with the continuous dialogue fostering a more supportive and growth-oriented team environment.

The action steps for Adobe's leaders included the following:

- **Regular Check-Ins:** Managers were trained to have frequent and informal conversations about goals, development, and performance with team members.

- **Clear Expectations:** Established clear expectations around goals, roles, and responsibilities at the start of the year.

- **Real-Time Feedback:** Encouraged giving and receiving feedback in real time, moving away from the traditional once-a-year review.

- **Focus on Growth:** Prioritized discussions on career development and opportunities for learning and personal growth.

- **Recognition and Reward:** Implemented systems to provide recognition and rewards that were tied to real-time achievements and contributions.

Adobe's Check-In framework demonstrates how fostering a culture of continuous development, feedback, and recognition can lead to a more engaged and motivated workforce, thus driving better business results and a stronger team spirit.

Many leading companies like Microsoft, Amazon, KPMG, Salesforce etc. view their investment in personal growth as a strategic business move. The benefits include increased employee engagement, higher retention rates, a more skilled and adaptable workforce, and often, a significant competitive advantage in their respective industries. This holistic approach to employee development reflects a shift in corporate culture towards valuing employee wellbeing and long-term career growth, which can in turn drive business success. For example, Google is renowned for its extensive employee development programs. They offer various personal growth opportunities, including skill workshops, mentorship programs, and internal mobility options. The effect is a highly skilled, motivated workforce that drives innovation and maintains Google's status as a tech leader. This investment is seen to attract and retain top talent and foster a culture of continuous learning and innovation.

Accenture also offers a wide range of learning opportunities, including training courses and a massive online learning platform. The result is a workforce that's constantly updating its skills and adapting to new market demands. Accenture invests in these programs to maintain a highly skilled consulting workforce and adapt quickly to client needs across a diverse array of industries.

Support Your Team's Personal Growth

What if you work in an organization that lacks the financial capacity for a unique learning platform? You can use external sources like *Udemy*, *Coursera*, *LinkedIn Learning*, or *Mindvalley*, just a few of many platforms that bring about growth and teach new skills. With the following simple method, you can ignite growth and increase awareness for the individuals responsible for kicking off their own values-based personal development.

Step 1: The 6 Magic Questions

In the first part of the book, you defined your 5D-Leadership purpose and aligned your own values with your company's values. You then thought about how to make these visible to your team and colleagues every day through your value-based words and actions. If you did this conscientiously, you've already experienced a significant change in your awareness and maybe even in your reality, because when your new beliefs and commitments lead to new behavior, those around you wonder why you're no longer acting *"like before"*. This is great if you've already received and acted on feedback! Keep up the good work. Now you can invite your employees to embark on a similar journey to become their *"best selves"*:

Setting the Stage

Invite your team at a time when it's a little quieter, depending on how your day-to-day business is organized. Turn off all phones, as disruptions should be avoided during the next 45-minute meeting. After sharing your leadership vision, ask the following questions to each individual, allotting 3–5 minutes to each person's answer:

1. What do I want to stand for? How do my values align with the company's values?

2. How do I want to contribute to the success of my team?

3. How can I create more magical moments in the team every day?

4. How do I want to contribute beyond my team and to the organization's growth?

5. What do I want to experience in my personal life? What goals do I want to achieve?

6. What is my strategy to achieve my newly defined goals in my own life?

You can ask your team if they want to share their answers openly, which is the ideal scenario. However, it may take some time (or a few trailblazers) to start the sharing process.

With these 6 *Magic Questions*, you don't only engage with your team on a personal level, but also show genuine interest in their personal development and learn what really interests them. It's fun to answer these questions, which reveal new insights about the team. When the questions are shared among the team, team members learn from each other as well. My experience is that from that moment on, when everyone sees each other in a newly holistic light, it changes a team positively forever; certain barriers are removed. With a simple task, you can create awareness that every soul has individual desires and wishes to contribute.

"Trust is the highest form of human motivation. It brings out the very best in people."

— STEPHEN COVEY

With the 6 *Magic Questions*, you can make your team members feel fully recognized as they realize their personal growth and development is desired by the employer. People rarely share their career goals openly. Because, when these career aspirations aren't met, employees get frustrated and may quit their jobs. If they don't, because they're too comfortable or feel tied down, they're likely to become less productive in their role. Transparency about personal goals helps to raise alternative development opportunities within the organization. Some people strive to deepen their skills and become more self-confident rather than focusing on growing their careers, because personal development is multi-dimensional and not one-sided. That's why you should regularly check the pulse of your team to identify any tensions.

Step 2: The Team Spirit Checkup

With the following *Team Spirit Checkup*, you'll discover unconscious weaknesses in the team, how they collaborate, how openly they communicate, how they support each other's growth, and how open they are to seeking help from others.

Measure the Spirit that Matters

When I started as a Co-CEO to work at our company ... *and dos Santos*, I was inspired by Keith Ferrazzi's *Leading Without Authority* and the way he inspired his team members through open and crisp questions. I became curious, and the next day, I sent this *"team spirit"* test to my team. We were – not positively – amazed at how mediocre we rated our team performance in some areas! As a result, we had to find solutions on how we could improve and discussed them thoroughly; half a year later, we'd significantly improved our results. Now, with a larger team, I regularly use this checkup to get an impression of where the team stands, how consistently we're aligned with a common vision, and how well we support each other to be successful. Many of my coaching clients also told me that this test changed the team spirit instantly.

The first checkup result is just a status; the more *"raw and real"* you get with the data, the easier it is to develop growth strategies based on this reality. Any *Team Spirit Checkup* status, even the lowest, can be accepted and used as a starting point for growth.

Preparation

My recommendation for the *Team Spirit Checkup* is to send the questionnaire by email or post it with a rating matrix from 1 (lowest) to 5 (highest) on your team platform. You should receive the answers back within three to five days. Present and discuss the results at the next team meeting, allowing room for discussion and an initial brainstorming session on how to level up together.

You can carry out the checkup every six months or annually, depending on the dynamics of the team. If your *Team Spirit Checkup* results stagnate or even fall, you can bring in a professional coach to run a joint workshop and help the team uncover the unconscious blocks to their own development and finally find ways to grow.

The Team Spirit Checkup

Send the following 10 questions to your team, rating them from 1 (lowest) to 5 (highest):

1. Do we feel we're communicating openly with strength and in a spirit of mutual support and dedication to our company's vision and our shared purpose?
2. Are we feeling truly connected and united in our efforts, and do we see the tangible benefits that come from our shared respect and reliance on each other's unique contributions?

3. Do we each feel a sense of responsibility for our unique commitments, and do we encourage each other to meet those commitments, working hand in hand to achieve our shared goals together?

4. Are we nurturing our collective growth by embracing learning experiences together and supporting each other through peer-to-peer coaching?

5. Are we uplifting each other's spirits and elevating our energy by celebrating our accomplishments and expressing our gratitude?

6. Are we leading generously, cultivating an environment of care and trust, and actively fostering supportive connections among us?

7. Are we lifting each other to reach new heights, nurturing an environment of innovation, and fostering transformation, rather than remaining content with the status quo?

8. Are we strategically building fruitful partnerships with those whose support and input can make a significant difference to our shared success?

9. Do we create magical moments in our team every day to strengthen our team spirit and enjoy working together?

10. What are your key ideas to elevate our team spirit to the next level?

Create a dynamic environment that values ongoing development and recognition. Sometimes there are team members that are unwilling to contribute to the team's success; you have to dive deeper into the conversation with them. The next tool may help you further.

Step 3: Evaluate the Frequency and Productivity of Your Team Members

With the last tool I'll introduce in this chapter, you can find out in direct 1:1 conversation with your employees how they rate their own performance in terms of their productivity for the company – but also what contribution they make to creating a positive mood and boosting the team's prevailing energy. These two key performance indicators can be viewed very differently, as there are very productive employees who nevertheless ruin the atmosphere with their constant nagging and spreading of bad vibes. This can affect the productivity of the whole team! There are countless ways to evaluate employees. Some calculate numerical values, some evaluations are done behind closed doors via multiple-choice questions, and other companies prefer direct employee interviews (which is also my preference). People can develop and change their behavior through higher awareness.

The Frequency and Productivity Matrix

This Matrix gives you a tool to discuss individual behavior from a new perspective and commit to an individual development plan for your team members.

Some people are low performers who make others feel great; others are *Toxic Achievers*, whose high performance and intense vibes make it difficult for positive frequencies to emerge through their negative behavior. This second type may be bitter because of a personal experience, disrupting the team and lowering the enjoyment of work with negative thoughts, gossip, and constantly drawing attention to the bad. They may have already quit inside and are looking for confirmation, or they can do the job left-handed and are consequently bored.

On the other hand, there are those who spread a great atmosphere but don't contribute strongly to good results; these are the *Energetic Underachievers*. The *Demotivating Drifter* represents individuals who not only fail to deliver results but also negatively impact the team's morale. Their lack of enthusiasm and persistent pessimism can make it difficult for the team to stay motivated and focused. In contrast, the *Positive Powerhouse* is the ideal team member who excels in their tasks while simultaneously uplifting the team's spirit. Their high productivity, combined with their ability to inspire and energize others, creates a thriving and dynamic work environment that fosters success and collaboration.

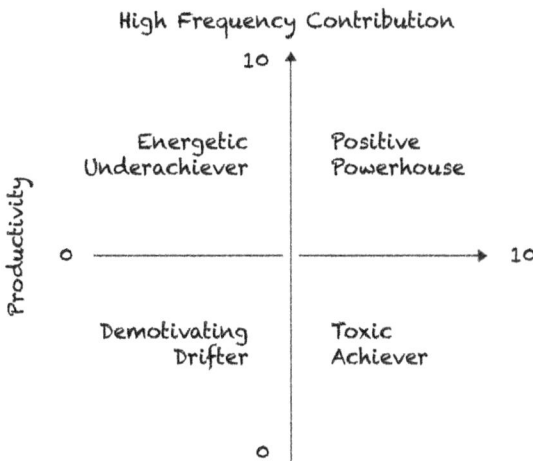

High Frequency Contribution

```
                          10 ↑

          Energetic            Positive
          Underachiever        Powerhouse

  Productivity
               0 ─────────────┼──────────────→ 10

          Demotivating         Toxic
          Drifter              Achiever


                           0 │
```

Therefore, this matrix, which was originally developed by the serial entrepreneur Eric Edmeades, is a very good tool to make an assessment with your employee regarding not only which level of productivity they see themselves as achieving, but also their frequency and positive energy contribution, and their role in the strengthening of morale and the overall will to win. Let's have a look at how the *Frequency & Productivity Matrix* works.

How to Use the Frequency & Productivity Matrix

In a 1:1 meeting with your team member, share the matrix with them and let them assess where they see themselves:

1. **How do you see your productivity from 0 to 10 on the horizontal axis?** 5 means *"on target"*, so there's a lot of room for over- and underperformance. Give them time to reflect, then ask them to list examples from their everyday work for their assessment. What makes them productive (+5 and above) and what slows them down (0 to 4)?

2. **How is your contribution in terms of high vibes and positive energy to the team? How do you level up our team spirit and help fulfil the overall vision? Where on the vertical from 0 to 10 do you see yourself?**
   Everything from 0 to 5 is *"below the line"* behavior, while scoring above 5 is exemplary.

Most of the time, it's the *Toxic Achievers* who get good results in terms of productivity, but push the mood hard, making them the most dangerous people in the team for destroying the spirit. Prepare yourself thoroughly for these conversations in order to have concrete examples of *"below the line"* behavior. Stay emotionally neutral and simply ask: What needs to happen for you to take on a higher frequency? Ask open questions to guide the employee towards a solution, such as:

- What is the benefit for you and the team if you change your behavior?

- What do you need to feel better and make others feel better?

- What do you need to stop doing to diminish your negative influence?

For those with low productivity:

- How can you increase your productivity?

- What do you need to start doing to achieve positive results?

- How can you achieve that?

An honest and consistent conversation triggers a reaction that needs to be monitored. Sometimes, the first reaction you cause isn't positive. Maybe your team member is already frustrated, so this conservation could be a trigger. There's no need to avoid conflict – find out the reason for this person's low vibes and ask them what they need to become more positive. Do they need change in their business or in their private life? Let them find the solution for themselves, insisting on a positive contribution. When people who drag the mood down choose to leave, it's often very liberating for the other team members. Some *Energetic Underachievers* can become *Positive Powerhouses* who need a good team culture to fully blossom.

Conditions for Success

This conscious work with the team, especially when it comes to personal issues, life experiences, and relationships, is only possible with the personal consent of the employee. It requires a relationship of trust, and can also enable a new, deeper level of trust. I've seen fantastic transformations in people, because feeling appreciated by a supportive leader is strongly correlated with personal growth.

Exceptional team spirit happens when trust, authenticity and empathy are lived out. Being an inspired 5D-Leader means that you've committed to the purpose of the company, aligned your values with the company's own, and exemplified this through action. Become the driving force for personal growth in your organization. You're dedicated to supporting the development of your team members, which you allow them to define on their own terms. Discussing consciousness in this way requires mindful moments, which create space for open conversations and provide time for reflection. Use these tools to create an inspiring, loving, and caring team atmosphere, and your people will care and love the company in return. Have frequent discussions with your team members and share constructive feedback in real time.

Summary of 4 Key Steps to Elevate Extraordinary Team Spirit

Become the champions of your team's personal development, linking personal fulfillment with professional success. Invest in your people's growth, as it not only enhances individual lives but also elevates the team spirit and overall business performance.

Step 1: Utilize the 6 Magic Questions

Implement these to understand and support employee aspirations and align them with the company's mission.

Step 2: Conduct the Team Spirit Checkup

Regularly evaluate team dynamics and address areas for improvement to foster trust and collaboration.

Step 3: Influence Your Team's Frequency & Productivity

Implement systems like the *Frequency & Productivity Matrix* to provide recognition of those who contribute positively to the vibes of the team, identifying those that influence the mood and help raise your team members' productivity.

Step 4: Use Regular Check-ins

Have frequent and informal conversations about goals, development, and performance with your team and give real-time feedback.

End of Part 2

With this chapter, we've completed ELEVATING 5D-LEADERSHIP CONSCIOUSNESS and learned how to ignite a positive mindset shift in your team. You're consequently able to support the personal growth of your team, using a range of tools and methods to increase productivity and intensify collaboration.

Now, let's turn to the topic BOOSTING INNOVATION WITH COLLECTIVE INTELLIGENCE. Collective intelligence helps your team grow vertically at an unprecedented rate. Your team can be phenomenal experts in their area, but experts are also those who tell you exactly how things can't be done! This slows down creativity and innovation. So, you need disruptive, diverse external input to truly break through and think in new ways. The innovator's dilemma lies in the foundations of an organization; over time, one develops operational blindness. Only new vibrations and confrontation with fresh thought patterns can dissolve old ones. Collective intelligence ignites inspiration; when applied consistently and skillfully, this creates actionable and effective innovative solutions by augmenting internal with external expertise. At the same time, collective intelligence accelerates transformation, encouraging people to part with the old and welcome the new. Let's now dive into the third part of the book, starting with the symphony of thought leaders that will help your team accelerate their transformational growth process.

BOOSTING INNOVATION WITH COLLECTIVE INTELLIGENCE

ORGANIZATIONAL TRANSFORMATION

CHAPTER 7

THE SYMPHONY OF THOUGHT LEADERS

Designing collective intelligence to accelerate transformation

*"Collective intelligence is the art of maximizing
simultaneously creative freedom and collaborative efficiency.
It's the capacity of human collectives to engage in intellectual
cooperation in order to create, innovate, and invent."*

— PIERRE LÉVY

I n the bustling concert of the modern workplace, the most harmonious symphonies aren't composed solo, but through the
collective intelligence of an orchestra of minds.
Collective intelligence is the ensemble of intellectual cooperation
where diverse individuals unite to innovate, create, and invent.
It's the art of orchestrating a multitude of perspectives, knowledge

bases, and problem-solving strategies to accelerate transformation and foster groundbreaking ideas. You can use collective intelligence in many different ways.

Take, for instance, the collaborative genius behind Wikipedia. No single author could pen such a voluminous and expansive repository of knowledge. Instead, it thrives on the contributions of thousands, each adding a note to the symphony of shared understanding.

Or consider the open-source marvel that is Linux, an operating system kernel that powers the majority of servers on the planet. Its development emerges from the keystrokes of developers worldwide, harmonizing their individual expertise into robust and versatile technology. You can also create an internal symphony by using a collective for communal creations or open-source landscapes, orchestrating the varied talents within a company.

Pixar Animation Studios exemplifies this beautifully within a corporate setting via their ideation sessions, where storytellers and animators gather not in competition, but in concert. They pitch, critique, and refine ideas, ensuring that the final movie is not just a story, but a saga that resonates with audiences of all ages.

Think about Google Maps and how they use the wisdom of crowds, bringing computers and groups of people working effectively together. Or think about Lego and how they work with people all over the world through *"Lego Ideas"*, inviting people to submit innovative ideas or new products for design.

Starbucks is also a great example of a company that's successfully implemented collective intelligence to drive innovation when they launched their *"Innovation Lab"* in 2018, propelling ideas from foundation to fruition in just one hundred days. This has resulted in hundreds of successful projects that are relevant to their customers, inspiring to their partners, and meaningful to their business. The platform collects ideas submitted directly from employees, allowing a safe space to create ideas. (*"Nitro Cold Brew"* is one of these bestsellers.) These examples underscore the essence of collective intelligence and its versatility. Whichever path you want to take, whether you work with crowd intelligence or selected thought leaders, you always need a systematic approach to achieve reliable results.

In this chapter, I'm focusing on the strategies that leverage your team's collective intelligence, transforming the solo performances of individual thought leaders into a grand symphony of innovation. If you believe in the power of *we* over *I*, you can ignite collective intelligence within your team to unlock their creative and inventive potential. This chapter equips you to harness your team's collective knowledge and create an inspiring new environment that champions co-creation for lasting success. It highlights how embracing diversity in thought encourages risk-taking and inclusivity, leading to quicker change. Additionally, it critiques traditional linear and process-focused approaches, suggesting that they underuse the innovative capacity of the brain. By fostering a *collective genius* with internal and external expertise, your team will unlock and utilize new cognitive areas, embracing different viewpoints and personal growth, which in turn energizes the company. Let's dive deeper and attune our minds to the rhythm of *collective genius*!

INSTALL A PERPETUUM FOR INNOVATION

Why do companies need constant innovation? There are essentially three things needed to optimize the customer experience, so that customers enthusiastically buy, use, recommend, and repurchase any company's products and services:

1. **Product Innovation:** Development of new products and services is essential, because technological progress constantly changes people's needs. It's a self-created cycle since the dawn of mankind, from tools to fire to the wheel, with every technological development awakening new needs and changing culture.

2. **Cultural Transformation:** Optimizing the employer experience, so that employees can develop to their full potential within the company and a culture of collaboration emerges to increase efficiency and innovation. Remember the company's cohesion, organism, heartbeat, soul, and purpose should be in alignment to energize humans; as described in the last chapters, you need to nurture cultural change constantly.

3. **Operational Excellence:** Making the system more efficient through automation, restructuring, introducing new systems and processes, and scaling for increased profitability, to be capable of investing in innovation and new segments.

Any company should constantly evolve and expand at all levels, which is the perpetual condition of innovation. If too many systems are blocked and fail, a company ages to its death. Use collective intelligence as a constant driver of innovation. In the following example, you can see what it takes to unleash the full potential of superheroes. Because even they face the challenge of not fully utilizing their talents until they agree on a common goal and become aware of their collective power!

The Symphony of Thought Leaders and Superheroes

Why does it take the power of a *collective genius* to achieve the extraordinary? Let's look at how superheroes do it.

Take the Avengers, a team of supernatural individuals with different abilities and personalities. Initially, their ego conflicts and different points of view lead to a lack of unity among them, thus reducing their efficiency. Iron Man, with his brilliant intellect and vast resources, is used to taking command and working on his own terms; he initially thinks only alone can he succeed. But it's only when he and the others put their egos aside and recognize the need to work together that they become a powerful force against their opponents!

At the same time, the Avengers learn that effective teamwork requires respect for each other's unique abilities. Each member, from the strength of the Hulk to the tactical acumen of Black Widow, contributes significantly to their collective victories. The realization that the team's success depends on the success of each member, not just one or two, solidifies the team's cohesion and effectiveness, and together they save humanity. The superhero stories we grew up with taught us to value other people and cultures and to treasure the differences between us. Only villains are xenophobic, racist, sexist, and hateful.

Spider-Man creator Stan Lee said,

"Racism and bigotry are among the deadliest social ills plaguing the world today."

Superheroes demonstrate how different cultures and appearances can work together for peace. They're trailblazers for diversity, inclusion, and the need for belonging. When they unite their superpowers in harmony, then play in a symphony, everything changes! Now, let's see how the X-Men ignite their collective forces. These superhuman mutants, who all have very different abilities, initially have difficulty uniting due to personal grudges and differing ideologies. Consider how diverse they are: Professor X masters telepathy. He can read minds, project his thoughts into the minds of others, and manipulate memories. Wolverine has superhuman strength, enhanced senses, and a regenerative healing factor that allows him to recover from virtually any wound. He also has retractable adamantium claws, while Cyclops emits powerful energy blasts from his eyes, which are uncontrollable without the aid of special eyewear. Or take Storm, a master of weather manipulation who can control atmospheric conditions. Their superpowers are unique, with many of them going through traumatic life experiences that made them unable to build trust at first. They all need to learn how to collaborate effectively as a team and rely on each other's force. Only as a team and with their forces united can they change the world. Diversity is a huge force.

These examples illustrate that collective power goes beyond individual capabilities. The key for leaders is to create an environment in which the unique strengths of each team member are recognized and leveraged toward a common goal. As these superhero teams demonstrate, the road to shared victory is paved with mutual respect, effective communication, discussions, a willingness to compromise, and an understanding that the whole is indeed greater than the sum of its parts. All must put their masks and egos aside.

Creativity Requires Respect, Diversity, Inclusion and Belonging

The natural gift of creativity is often underdeveloped by today's management style, which is in many cases more efficiency- and process-oriented. As a result, creative thinking needs to be encouraged to develop new solutions. Most managers' career paths are very linear, often predefined by what they need to achieve, as well as how much sales and marketing or strategic and financial experience they need to get promoted. These repeating patterns create more operational blindness, strengthening the own immune system that opposes change *"from experience"*. Furthermore, these career paths are very competitive – you must be faster, smarter, and above all better-networked to gain those rare positions at the top. Creative employees who may have less career ambition often feel inferior to such stringent, career-oriented managers, but their expertise is crucial for solving internal problems; *"fear relationships"* with top management block the free, open, creative, and abstract thinking necessary to work together towards innovative, smart, workable, and meaningful solutions.

It's indeed difficult to establish this "let's release our egos and collaborate for a common goal" in an organization with competing managers, due to the hierarchical structures. How can you disrupt this? Start with yourself. Be a guiding light, proud to make a difference. If you decide to use collective intelligence to arrive at better ideas, observe how often you push down others' opinions and ideas far too early based on your "gut feeling" or "expert knowledge", instead of taking the time to let data prove whether the idea was right or wrong.

Regardless of what superpowers you have, the linear thinking that's required for thinking in hierarchical structures and processes unconsciously encourages you to freeze in your fixed thought patterns. If you want to make far-reaching decisions, you need ambitious, flexible thinkers who take on brain-teasers without management, and who have sound experience and broad knowledge of the business area you want to transform. A variety of diverse perspectives enables complex challenges to be tackled that can't be solved alone.

Collective Intelligence Design with External Expertise

Designing collective intelligence is an art. It takes a great deal of knowledge and understanding of people and their motivations, as well as the needs, mechanics, and cultures of organizations, to steer complex issues towards a common goal within a team of distinct thinkers of diverse backgrounds, skills, opinions, and perspectives. A *collective genius* needs the freedom to work things out, with an emphasis on openness to new solutions rather than relying on planned results. The creative power a collective can develop when it pulls together to elaborate and implement ideas is exponentially higher than in a team of linear thinkers.

When your team learns to collaborate effectively with a group of new, diverse team members, it has a positive impact in many ways. The extraordinary inspiration opens their minds to new ideas and new people, so that next time they can approach their colleagues more openly; this increases the chances of achieving shared goals. Often, fears of rejection or suppression of one's own ideas by other colleagues block the way forward. When people realize that they can proactively break down silos, accept different perspectives, find compromises, and create something greater together than originally expected, this provides lasting encouragement for new approaches and boosts overall energy.

Using collective intelligence is a smart way to develop creative, well-thought-through decisions. Of course, just putting a bunch of different people together in a room won't work; instead, you need to guide their thinking process to create extraordinary results. I'll explain this process in the next chapter – but first, let's dive a bit deeper into how our brain functions on a basic level, which will help you gain more insight and perspective when selecting the right thought leaders for the task you're aiming to solve.

The Human Brain

In order to unleash innovation that stands up to competitors, you should create a collective with the aim of fully utilizing the human capacity (and brain capacity) of the thought leaders. Keep in mind the human brain, with the different functions of its left and right hemispheres. The following illustration is extremely simplified, while the brain's activities are highly interconnected. Nonetheless, the following overview of the key areas associated with each hemisphere gives you an idea that you need both hemispheres fully engaged to create innovative and balanced solutions:

Left Brain

- **Language skills:** Includes speaking, writing, reading, and understanding language.
- **Logical thinking:** Involves analytical abilities and sequential processing.
- **Mathematical abilities:** Skills in calculations and understanding numbers.
- **Fact retention:** Good at remembering facts and details.
- **Linear thinking:** Processes information in a linear, methodical manner.

Right Brain

- **Creative thinking:** Involves imagination, artistic abilities, and innovation.
- **Spatial ability:** Understanding of space, distance, and size.
- **Intuition:** Involves gut feelings and sensing things without explicit reasoning.
- **Holistic thinking:** Seeing the bigger picture and thinking in terms of overall patterns.
- **Emotional perception:** Recognizing and interpreting emotions in others.

Left Brain
INVENTION

Right Brain
EXPANSION

Language

Logic

Mathematics

Sequencing

Experimentation

Facts

Control

Stability

Order

Creativity

Dimensions

Community

Intuition

Imagination

Arts

Uncertainty

Universality

Feelings

internal

external

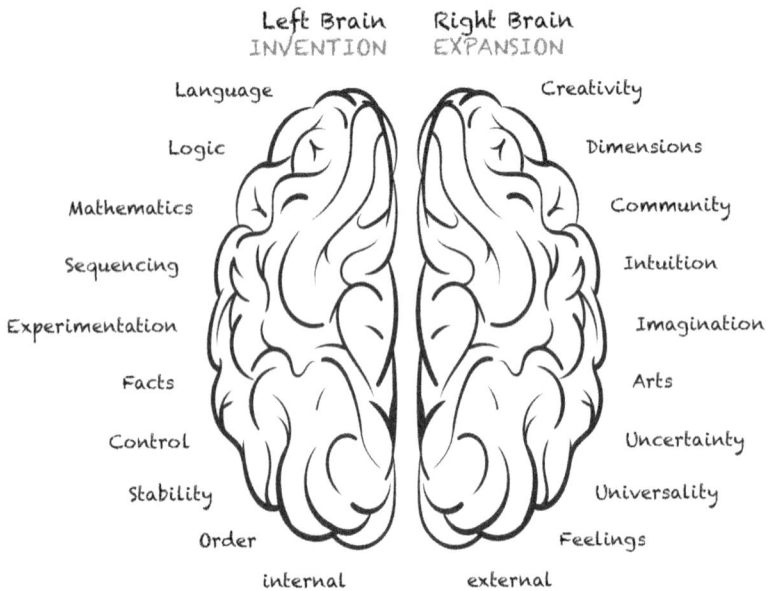

While looking at the illustration, reflect on the role of each hemisphere for certain roles in your organization. In a management context, for instance, both hemispheres of the brain are ideally fully utilized (although the specific challenges of a managerial role may dictate which hemisphere is more actively engaged). In management, the left brain is useful for tasks involving logic, such as budgeting, planning, setting goals, and analyzing data. The ability to methodically process information is crucial in making reasoned decisions and managing day-to-day operations. Conversely, the right brain is important for creative roles and leadership positions requiring emotional intelligence and big-picture thinking. Skills including empathy, team-building, innovative problem-solving, and strategic visioning are associated with right-brain activities.

How Many of Today's Roles Force Us to Use our Brain in Unbalanced Ways

Ideally, job roles are designed to strengthen the balanced use of both left- and right-brain skills. That's not the case, though, because job roles are designed not for humans, but for the tasks that need to be done. Think about people who handle machines, computers, or robots all day: Which part of the brain will they use more proactively to fulfill their tasks? Or consider clerks with a financial and analytical role that rarely requires any creativity. Which parts do they activate naturally for their work? On the other hand, how much analytical skill do graphic designers need during the day? How do they hone their language skills through their work? When you create a team of graphic designers, how do you find balance? Similarly, how do you balance out clerks? The ability to analyze data and approach problems logically (left-brain skills) while also being creative, empathetic, and visionary (right-brain skills) makes a well-rounded and effective leader. We are individuals, so *how* we use our brain depends on the specific demands of the job profile, industry, or organizational culture, as there are many differences between the construction, automotive, food, fashion, IT, finance, or consultancy industries, for example.

Creating a Collective Innovation Brain

When you're designing a collective intelligence, you should take the necessary hemispheres of the innovation brain into account and consciously bring together creative, empathetic, and intuitive people with logical, fact-oriented and analytical thinking minds. Together, they're more likely to find different, smarter, and more innovative or even disruptive solutions.

Next to the different brain hemispheres, another perspective is based on people's vertical development, and in what dimension of reality their consciousness resides. People with higher awareness are energetically balanced, open for discussion, empathetic, collaborative, eager to learn from others, and inspired by new ideas. 5D-Leaders are open to advancing to the next level by learning from others, from their success as well as from their failures. They're eager to make the most of every second of the day, and while they're respectful and self-confident, they also invite others to grow rather than suppressing their ideas; hence, they have the ideal mindset for co-creation.

When you search for ideal experts to awaken your team, search for versatile people with profound experience who can confront current structures and break old thinking patterns. Often, it needs an extra portion of innovative support to give the crazy ideas you were unsure about a more solid foundation. Collective intelligence is best used for creative sessions, like developing new business models, mastering interdisciplinary projects, and elaborating transformative solutions. Just think about what kind of expertise your team needs – and now think really big and just look for the best. Because true masters have a higher vibrational frequency and can easily animate others. Whether it's a specialist in certain technologies like AI, robots or blockchain; or a certified psychologist or neuroscientist; maybe a successful serial entrepreneur and start-up CEO; or even an Academy Award winner or sports champion; or an MIT professor or a female multi-supervisory board member. Choose challenging experts that are suited to fit your needs and have the knowledge and experience that your employees lack. Of course, you can start on a smaller scale or even without any external professional support, but you'll benefit by having the courage and conviction to choose qualified and well-experienced thought leaders that bring much-needed expertise to the table and can look far beyond the usual horizons of your team.

Developing innovative and transformative solutions requires assembling essential building blocks. One is the *collective genius*, carefully selected according to clear principles and prerequisites based on the current needs described above. Another block is the design-focused thought process towards the solution, again depending on the task at hand. I'll explain the design of this approach and the thought process in the next chapter – but first, let's see how to ensure your collective's character creates an inspiring symphony of voices.

Designing the Character of a Collective Genius

For example, with the think tank of ... *and dos Santos*, we've developed the concept of an unusual and important future workplace, the cockpit of an upcoming new High-Speed Train model, for the largest European railroad company. This new *"ICE"* High-Speed Train is scheduled to run on rails from 2031 onwards. There will still be train drivers on European rails for the next three decades (and probably more) – although High-Speed Trains drive more and more automatically, they won't operate fully autonomously. In an industry where products such as High-Speed Trains have a service life of thirty years, far-reaching changes have to be planned through and through, many years in advance.

For the development of this future High-Speed Train cockpit, we needed, in addition to our client's internal train experts, a diverse team that was familiar with digitalization, automation, future workplace design, and next-level technical solutions with a focus on rolling stock and mobility.

Next to the participating train drivers, we needed scientists, makers, and creative, open-minded innovators. In the project's initial phase, we'd already analyzed key functionalities and design principles for this future workplace, based on best practices from the rail industry (as well as other benchmarked industries like aerospace or shipping). Compared to aviation, the European railroad industry is more bound to its old structures, less innovative and standardized. To select the right lab team, we were therefore looking for experts with experience from different industries who were also able to engage and argue at a high technical level, while bringing knowledge of "New Work" and the needs of the next generation who'll ultimately take control of the future trains into play. "New Work" is primarily focusing on the evolving nature of work in the contemporary economic and social landscape but also about rethinking the essence of work itself to foster environments that prioritize personal satisfaction, economic efficiency, and sustainable practices. It's an evolving concept that responds to the necessities and opportunities of the modern world, aiming to redefine societal structures for the betterment of all individuals.

We selected a very diverse team, a Visual Effects Oscar® winner who's been working with immersive technologies, and on various VR simulation concepts for High-Speed Train cockpits and aeronautic designs; a PhD in Human Interface Design who's experienced with automated streetcars, and who worked on a project for teleoperated driving of cars in big cities; a serial start-up CEO and creative who's been working on a variety of future projects like central utility services such as energy, water, electricity, and public transport for the German capital of Berlin, as well as having strong tech-related relationships with Japan and Singapore, which have advanced train systems; and a leading university professor of artificial intelligence and digital transformation at work.

We had to invest in the collective to build a common starting point for all parties. To do this, we provided them with the research results, then let them peruse current High-Speed Train cockpit designs in detail. As well, we shared examples of "good" and "bad" experiences train drivers had shared with us, coupled with their key requirements. These experiences had been compiled by the train drivers participating in the project. All experts were taken on a journey in the driver's cab of a modern *ICE* High-Speed Train to experience what activities a train driver has to carry out and how they currently handle the technical equipment, which communication channels they can use, and how high the degree of networking and technological standard of their systems are. The external experts served as the inspiration, and they were challenging the train drivers' findings where appropriate. We had a lot of controversial discussions, and the concept is the result of true co-creation between internal and external masters. The core work was done by the train drivers themselves. Thanks to the in-depth analyses performed, the inspirational *"springboards"* we developed, and above all, the targeted questioning of the experts in our collective, we were able to develop a comprehensive and groundbreaking new concept that's already had a major influence on the redesign of the future workplace.

At the beginning of this challenging project, I was skeptical that we could achieve an innovative breakthrough that would be recognized by international train designers and technical experts alike, while simultaneously considering the diverse human needs of tomorrow's train drivers. Technical innovation must move in tandem with human demands, such as smart information systems that support the driver's work. By providing a collaborative environment of diverse thinkers while contributing rich knowledge-based resources, our client was able to unleash the deep wisdom of their team to create an unimagined blueprint for a future High-Speed Train cockpit. The concept has already attracted a great deal of international attention for the requirements of a future workplace and has been incorporated into the development of the new *ICE* train for 2031. This project was one of a series of five for which we were awarded the global Bold Award for the Future of Work.

Agile Methods Require Discipline

On the one hand, success is about finding the best match in terms of expertise, but it's also about uniting diverse brains and personality types in such a way that different thinking preferences seamlessly come together. For engineers and systems-based thinkers, engaging with creatives, artists, and free thinkers encourages new ways of thinking. On the other hand, agile methods – for example, a design-based thought process with an individual *collective genius* – need a considerable amount of discipline, otherwise it's easy to get bogged down. The stability in the process allows flexibility.

Building *collective genius* means making people more important than ideas, suggesting that achieving the ideal team-based chemistry can elevate or transform an average idea into something extraordinary. Believe in assembling teams of people who are smarter than you are, and understand that humility and trust in the team's capabilities are crucial for fostering an environment where great ideas can flourish. This includes viewing failure not as a necessary evil but as an integral part of the creative process, making quality a primary component of your business plan, and maintaining a flat communication structure where everyone can talk to each other without fear of reprimand. This open communication system is pivotal in creating a safe environment where individuals feel encouraged to take risks and share their work without fear of judgment.

The atmosphere in the collective allows candid feedback to be shared among peers in a structured yet non-hierarchical setting, elevating the creative output. When selecting the people, it helps to assess their interest in the challenge you're facing, their breadth of knowledge in the subject area, the degree of diversity they contribute to the collective, and their ability to work in a team on an equal footing. The discipline and mindfulness required at the instigation of an innovative project to unite complementary personalities, expertise, and cultural building blocks is guaranteed to be rewarded when the collective achieves a state of flow during their sessions.

7 Questions for the Assembling of a Collective Genius

1. What expertise does your own team bring to the table?
2. Which personalities are on the team? Researcher or reticent, questioner or formulator, extrovert or introvert, diplomat or commander, teacher or decision-maker, etc.?
3. What expertise is needed in terms of market, industry, product, processes, culture, stakeholders, target group and technology?
4. Which aspect of innovation do the people selected primarily use in solving their tasks? Do they take a balanced approach, or tend to be more creative or analytical?
5. What mindsets should the external experts adopt to maintain equilibrium within the group? Should they disrupt, confront, or clarify and prioritize?
6. When you've selected experts for their knowledge, check their level of grit, collaborative attitude, and personality. Then, consider how you can best create the desired character of the project with them (challenging, supporting, inspiring, etc.).
7. When you've selected the collective, think again. What skills does the leader of the project team need to have to hold all these masterminds together? How experienced should they be, and how much expertise about the project is necessary?

By harnessing the power of this type of collaborative intelligence, your team can tap into a wealth of knowledge and insights from a variety of sources. Doing this with care will help you form a team capable of enhancing creative thinking, disrupting old codes, and developing innovative solutions to each challenge that arises.

Why does the approach of using a external experts for innovation sometimes fail? "We've tried everything, we've worked with experts, a famous professor wanted to set us up with a think tank, but what we worked out in initial projects was never realized. Our responsible executives have very different opinions about how relevant digitization is, so we're only making small progress," the CMO of a German-based global security tech company told me. Traditionally managed companies are aware they're often lagging behind with innovation and digitization; the challenges have become increasingly complex due to the mounting global crisis, placing organizations and employees under increasing pressure. Why do so many good ideas and solutions get stuck in a drawer?

The 4 Main Pitfalls for Driving Innovation

1. **The immune system of a company,** which protects a well-established system from any risks.

2. **The inability to cooperate on an eye-to-eye level,** which often comes from managers who see dominance as a tool for leadership.

3. **The lack of stakeholder integration** right from the project's beginning.

4. **The quality of the experts.** You won't create great results with a mediocre team.

Of course, the challenges of creating innovation go much further and deeper than I can explain here by way of example; these four points only briefly reflect the causes of a lack of innovative strength within a company.

1. The Immune System

Many companies feel exhausted by the constant changes driven by the current global crisis and the speed of technological innovation. On top of this, each company's immune system blocks new thinking. Stability offers safety; that's a natural process, nothing unusual. However, companies need to become aware of this immune system, then look at it with a critical eye. Recognize how innovations are actively prevented through *"yesterday's knowledge"*. New thinking and action can be practiced. Develop a culture of collaboration, start a transformation program, and get external help if needed. You'll have to take this challenge seriously to become future-ready and to break through old, rigid thought patterns.

2. Unbiased Collaboration

Co-creation is a participatory process that is openly demanded by the younger generation. But older employees also want to be involved in the decision-making process, especially when it comes to their future areas of work. True co-creation requires an attitude of humility to ensure that the views of all participants have equal weight. This humble behavior in discussions and brainstorming processes is often not easy, especially for traditional strategy consultants, who have learned to dominate others by flaunting the power of their knowledge, leading the client with eloquent language, and underpinning their own intelligence by constantly questioning others.

This behavior is often not meant maliciously, but simply force of habit; after all, you were brought in for a job to solve problems quickly. However, co-creation isn't about knowing better, but about collaboration.

Such tactics are ineffective, however, because every person in the room has the right to express themselves openly and help shape things, even if they're less practiced in eloquent language or making rapid leaps of thought (given their job doesn't always require it).

3. Stakeholder Integration

The most important stakeholders from different departments must be involved in the process. This is time-consuming, laborious, and difficult – but it's necessary. I have over twenty-five years' experience as a leader of global companies with different cultural backgrounds. In every company environment, it's of utmost importance to get top management approval for the implementation of innovation projects and at the same time, a bottom-up approach is required to ensure that the idea is down-to-earth enough to be implemented through the employees' combined efforts. Plans hatched by those in power alone, and without further integration of the team, don't have a high chance of gaining acceptance within the company. Widespread participation is important, even if it's difficult to reach everyone who's involved or touched by the project or make them happy.

On the one hand, it's the carefully selected design of the collective and its detailed thought process that makes the difference. On the other, stakeholders from all affected areas must be involved in the process and proactively asked for their feedback; this must be considered from the outset when designing a solution if it's to have a chance of success.

4. Quality of the Experts

"If you give a good idea to a mediocre team, they will screw it up. If you give a mediocre idea to a brilliant team, they will either fix it or throw it away and come up with something better."

— EDWIN E. CATMULL,

Co-Founder of Pixar, President of Walt Disney Animation Studios

Choose the best people for the team tasked with creating innovative solutions. You need gifted minds to develop exceptional and sustainable concepts that don't remain in the drawer afterwards but actually get implemented. How are you supposed to put together a team of highly skilled thinkers if you don't have access to external expertise? In today's world, access to expertise is made much easier through technology. Use think tanks, external networks, or professional social platforms. LinkedIn, for example, the largest business network in the world with over 900 million members, offers direct access to outstanding experts of any kind, aided by a versatile search function. Universities offer their professors' contact details on their websites, and countless other associations and groups offer access to experts. Furthermore, many companies offer their employees the opportunity to work on external projects for a few days a year. This allows them to gain exciting insights and learn something new at the same time, and to learn new approaches and solutions from other managers from other sectors.

Summary of the Four Key Steps to Creating a Collective Genius

Step 1: Implement Constant Innovation

Think about how you can encourage your organization to be permanently innovative by installing collective intelligence as a tool for perpetual inspiration.

Step 2: Harness External Expertise

Use external networks, think tanks, and professional social network platforms to find external experts to introduce fresh perspectives and specialized knowledge to your team. Go beyond the well-known standards in your search for disruption.

Step 3: Design Collective Intelligence

Unlock higher creativity and problem-solving capabilities, allowing your team to release past thinking patterns and obsolete structures. To prepare the selection, complete the *"7 Questions for the Assembling of a Collective Genius"*.

Step 4: Agile Discipline

While agility is necessary for innovation, it requires discipline to avoid getting bogged down. A systematic assessment of team members' expertise, interest, collaborative skills, and diversity of thought is crucial for success, as is having a clear definition of the required expertise and building a balanced innovation brain.

Now you have a vision of how to create a symphony of thought leaders for growth. With the given advantages of a *collective genius* comes the requirement of an actionable framework and methodology for how collective intelligence can be systematically implemented within an organization's existing processes. Turn the page and let's dive into how to develop the collective thought process to design the thinking for a better tomorrow.

Chapter 8

DESIGN THINKING FOR A BETTER TOMORROW

Unleash creative innovation and ignite the collective Growth Zone

*"We moved from thinking of ourselves as designers to
thinking of ourselves as design thinkers.
We have a methodology that enables us to come up with
a solution that nobody has before."*

— DAVID KELLY,
Founder of IDEO

David Kelly, Professor at Stanford University and founder of IDEO and the Hasso Plattner Institute of Design, is considered one of the pioneers of the innovative design thinking method. His radical notion proposes that creativity can be summoned at will, via a process not unlike the scientific method.

He's convinced that practicing design unleashes unimaginable results and boosts people's creativity as well as confidence.

IDEO, with over 700 employees in nine offices across three continents, has applied Kelly's methodology to drive innovation, create 1,000+ patents since 1978, and win hundreds of design awards. It's the go-to design lab for curing innovation anemia for clients including Anheuser-Busch, Coca-Cola, Gap, Ford, HBO, Marriott, and more. Together with his friend Steve Jobs, Kelly developed Apple's first computer mouse. He's highly decorated, having received the National Design Award and been appointed Chair of the Stanford School of Engineering. Design thinking works perfectly across all branches, continents, and products.

Like Einstein, Kelly believes that creativity isn't the domain of a chosen few, but that *everyone* is creative. He believes that the natural ability to come up with new ideas, as well as the courage to try them out, is within each of us. His philosophy of design thinking aims to help people overcome the fears blocking their creativity, building confidence by succeeding in small steps. But there's more to it than simply unleashing creativity for all who use it.

Recent research published by Rahmin Bender-Salazar shows that design thinking isn't only an unmatched design method that educates people by using the process to boost creative and gain confidence. When applied in a model where inspiration, ideation, and solution implementation are followed by experimentation, iteration, and continuous learning, design thinking is an effective method for problem-solving, including complex and wicked problems. As McKinsey's research indicates, organizations that regularly follow design thinking practices see their revenues increase by a third, with 56 percent higher returns to shareholders compared to those that don't.

This suggests that design thinking can contribute to higher revenue and better shareholder returns.

In this chapter, I'll describe the principles of design thinking to explain how you can use this incomparably versatile method to trigger innovation, transformation, and growth for your employees and your company as a whole. I'll provide food for thought by showing various industry examples. Allow me to stick with the core principles, rather than going into depth about the method's possibilities, which would go far beyond the scope of this book.

For this reason, I'd like to invite you to reach a deeper insight into design thinking by recommending the excellent books by Michael Lerwick, whose *Playbooks on Design Thinking* explain the various approaches and tools in detail while revealing how to select the correct one depending on the task. Let me now bring this miraculous gift a little closer.

Design Thinking Changing the World

The principles of design thinking have changed our world, with Apple leading the way by showing itself to be a pioneer of the method; their focus on user-centered design and the seamless integration of hardware and software became a hallmark of their success. The introduction of iconic products like the iPod, iPhone, and iPad not only changed the way we interact with technology, but extensively influenced today's world. Other revolutionary companies, such as Airbnb, are using design thinking principles to address travelers' needs for unique, authentic experiences and hosts' desire for extra income, creating a platform that connects people in a new way. This success can be attributed to the company's deep understanding of both sides of the market. Amazon can't be left off this list, of course.

Jeff Bezos repeatedly emphasizes how important a customer focus is to him; as a result, the company is willing to experiment, take risks, and rethink based on customer feedback embodies design thinking principles.

If design thinking is such a universally successful method, why hasn't it long since been adopted by *all* companies?

Challenges for Traditional Companies

In traditional, hierarchical companies, working at eye level with each other in a multidisciplinary team is a big challenge. Implementing design thinking principles in complex organizations also involves winning stakeholders over to the idea. If you return from a creative design thinking session with your team, then share your great new idea, the first thing you experience is usually a strong headwind. Remember, the traditional company's immune system preventing change is usually strong. It prefers safe zones, and very quickly kills the many good ideas that were born in the *"protected space"* of the design thinking collective. If the company's not flexible and receptive to change, ambitious new ideas simply crash to earth. With so much time and money wasted, the status quo's defenders quickly blame the design thinking method instead of the outdated management system.

Organizations focused on efficiency and productivity work in silos. Within this strict hierarchy, employees are told what to do with few variables. Boredom, operational blindness, and linear thinking are too often the results. Remember, what disrupts these old structures and ways of thinking is new inspiration that demands consistent engagement. The easiest way to get someone out of their comfort zone is to confront them with other thinking minds – ideally thought leaders who are experiencing a different work-based reality, as well as being proven experts in their field and committed to helping others grow.

For something meaningful to emerge from such a collective, and for the team members to gain strength and self-confidence throughout the process, two key parameters are required (as described in the last chapter). The first is the carefully assembled collective of internal and external experts to boost innovation; the second is the design thinking approach, the systematic thought process.

PRINCIPLES OF DESIGN THINKING

Design thinking is a human-centered approach to problem-solving and innovation that involves understanding people's needs, developing creative ideas, and iterating solutions. This method encourages multidisciplinary collaboration, empathy, and a willingness to embrace ambiguity – all key components in the creation of disruptive solutions. The following principles form the basis of a successful design thinking process, and must be thoroughly considered before starting a so-called design lab:

· **Empathy:** Understanding the needs, emotions, and perspectives of the people involved lies at the core of this method. Empathy means putting yourself in the shoes of customers, employees, and stakeholders, actively listening to them, and observing their behavior to gain deep insights that inform the process. However, this is much more easily said than done! To enable this change of perspective, you need to prepare many insights about the target group, making them as lively as possible with videos, images, and quotes. (Choosing to take a different perspective based purely on abstract data analyses is highly unlikely.) In order for the project team to develop empathy, they also need detailed information enabling them to actively empathize with the target group. (This must be taken into account as inspiration during the preparation phase.) When we're asked to support an organizational change, we often start by developing the personas – and even the *future* personas – of those employees who'll be most affected by digitalization or generational change. This allows everyone involved to engage with the task far more personally.

- **Human-Centered Solutions:** People are at the center of this process, enabling meaningful problems to be tackled by creating solutions that align with the individual or target group's values, preferences, and desires. Make sure you thoroughly analyze and understand these before you start working on a solution.

- **Iteration:** A non-linear iterative process includes repeated cycles of brainstorming, prototyping, testing, and refining. Each iteration builds on the insights and findings of the previous one. Repetition and further development of content stimulates deeper understanding of problems, engaging broader thinking.

- **Collaboration:** As explained in the last chapter, cross-functional collaboration is critical. Diverse perspectives from different disciplines contribute to richer and more innovative solutions. Collaboration encourages the exchange of ideas and prevents isolated thinking, especially when sharing ideas with others.

· **Visualization:** Visualizing ideas and concepts helps communicate insights within a team and subsequently to key stakeholders. Sketches, diagrams, and prototypes allow complex ideas to be communicated easily. Visualization leads to more comprehensive deliverables that evoke emotion and empathy. Marketing teams love working with visuals, but this is rarer in the world of engineering or finance.

· **Open-mindedness:** This process encourages an open and non-judgmental mindset. All ideas are welcome, even those that may initially seem unconventional or unrealistic. Radical ideas can often lead to breakthrough solutions. Be aware of your company's immune system, which reflexively shoots down so-called *"crazy ideas"*.

· **Problem Reframing:** Before embarking on finding solutions, design thinking emphasizes the importance of thoroughly understanding the problem. This includes reframing the problem to ensure you're addressing the core challenge – not just the symptoms. Often considered tedious, this is a necessary step. Take the example of addressing high rates of workplace absenteeism. Initially, the problem may seem simple: Employees aren't coming to work. However, upon reframing, the problem could be understood as employees not feeling engaged or motivated. In this reframed understanding, solutions wouldn't focus on punitive measures for absenteeism but rather on improving workplace culture, offering flexible work options, or recognizing employee contributions. By reframing the problem, the solutions move from treating the symptom (absenteeism) to addressing a potential root cause (lack of engagement).

· **Prototyping:** Creating low-fidelity prototypes allows ideas to be visualized and tested quickly. Prototypes can be anything from sketches and storyboards to digital simulations. We often sketch future scenarios and create UX design drafts of new applications or storyboards, but this is also done for other conceptual frameworks (e.g. future job profiles, new business models).

· **Feedback and Testing:** Regular testing with end-users or stakeholders helps validate assumptions and gather feedback on prototypes. This iterative feedback loop ensures that the solution matches people's needs and can be refined accordingly. Watch out! Make sure you get detailed feedback during the development process, especially from relevant stakeholders.

· **Fail Fast, Learn Faster:** Design thinking embraces the idea that failure is a valuable part of the learning process. Act and learn. Early and frequent failure allows you to uncover mistakes, change course, and make improvements before com-mitting extensive resources. Especially in larger and traditional organizations, the idea of starting with an "MVP" – Minimal Viable Product – is understood but still needs repetition. As too many stakeholders want "perfect" solutions instead of simple ones, they often lack the imagination to understand that a first idea can evolve into an ideal solution. While software developers know this rule by heart, it can be applied to many work processes. There's still extensive resistance to this idea, as people lack the necessary imagination that simple solutions can evolve into very smart ones.

· **User Stories:** Creating personas and user stories helps take a user-centric approach. These outline the needs, goals, and behaviors of different types of users. In our workshops, we regularly find that if we create personas representing different types of employees, we gain in-depth and empathetic discussions. Stepping into one of these personas – for example, a trainee with a different ethnic background and a lack of language skills, or a seasoned leader and family man with twenty-six years' experience – makes it much easier to under-stand their different work-related needs and motivations. Personas help you step away from abstract discussions in favor of lively everyday situations. Listen to user stories of, for example, how they've experienced their employer's education system is often truly eye-opening, compared to discussing ab-stract case studies of other companies. A great example is the Cleveland Clinic's video "Empathy: The Human Connection to Patient Care", which creates a more caring and com-passionate hospital environment by placing healthcare professionals in the shoes of their patients and colleagues. We're all in the same situation – remember, every professional could become a patient tomorrow.

Creating Sustainable Change Through Design Thinking

By integrating these principles into your problem-solving approaches, you can harness the power of design thinking to find innovative solutions, strengthen team collaboration, and achieve transformation. When all phases – inspiration, ideation, implementation, and iteration – are played out, faster movement is the result. And remember, design thinking isn't a rigid formula, but a flexible framework that can be adapted to different contexts and challenges. So, what does the process look like? A complete lab process consists of four basic phases, which you can visualize as a cycle:

The 4 Key Steps of the Design Thinking Process

1. Inspiration
2. Ideation
3. Implementation
4. Iteration

Step 1: The Inspiration Phase

Start with the result in your mind, remembering that the ultimate goal you want to achieve is oneness. The result of the change you're aiming to initiate can be multi-faceted or multi-dimensional, solving your business problem on the one hand, but keeping in mind optimizing human and global wellbeing on the other. With this overarching perspective in mind, you can tackle any problem you face.

The inspiration phase begins with a deep dive in analytics. Include careful qualitative and quantitative data analysis, examine future trends, conduct empathic interviews with the target group to study people's deeper needs and motivations, hear their experiences, and gain new perspectives. Interweave interviews with stakeholders into the project's landscape, as well as drawing on external partners with profound knowledge. In addition to analyzing the status quo, prepare an overview of your chosen category's mega-trends and best practices across your industry. Introduce perspectives from influencers within the business community to help you escape the tunnel vision of your own data, opening up a wide vista of possibilities. The goal of this phase is to reframe the problem based on the human-centered principles listed above, then clearly define the task for the lab team. This requires a strong focus on guiding ideation from the beginning, in order to build common ground and manifest a shared vision.

At the end of this phase, you'll think about how to design the collective as described in Chapter 7. Consider your initial situation, your goal, the expertise you have on hand, and the required qualities of all participants. Experts should be curious, open-minded, and adaptable, while also willing to have their assumptions challenged. Carefully consider your team's makeup, aiming for a mix of mindsets, departments, skills, and perspectives. Then, design the collective, hire the external experts, and last but not least when you've reframed the problem, define the questions you want to get answered during the ideation workshop.

Step 2: The Ideation Phase

Start with a Briefing

Take the liberty of scheduling a briefing session a few days before the ideation workshop, tuning everyone into the exciting task at hand. The briefing gives weight to the task and offers an early opportunity for inspiration, preparing participants for the ideation workshop. We prepare so-called *"springboards"* for the group – first hypotheses of possible solutions and best practices based on the analysis and generated insights, which help the team head in the right direction during the first idea-generating session.

Run the Ideation Workshop

The ideation workshop is about finding ideas for the problem. All data, results, and even personas have been developed during the inspiration phase, with key principles for the solution often worked out here first. A wide variety of methods can be used in a workshop, as listed below – different techniques to elaborate the best possible idea. Deliberately seek confrontation and take time for reflection. Start the workshop with simpler tasks, then go deeper as the day goes on. After each brainstorming session, take the time to condense and prioritize the team's ideas. **What's relevant, and what can we leave out?** (This is often difficult for participants, but decisions must eventually be made.) Use e.g. voting tools for this task, while running the workshop on a visual collaboration platform like *Miro* or *Mural*.

Ideation workshops ideally combine creative work and often-painful insights with a sense of fun. To get in the right mood, it helps when many people come together that don't know each other well to use icebreakers like 'One Truth, Two Lies', or designing a colleague's avatar are great openers. There are many templates available (at Miro.com, for example); choose the one that best fits your group. The ideation workshop's key task is to move from your initial inspiration, the abstract analysis and insights, towards an ideation of ideas and a synthesis, which could include testing various hypotheses that could lead to a solution.

During the workshop, consider using the following methods to create a hypothesis:

- **Inspiration:** Mentally stimulate the team to do or feel something (especially something creative) with videos, visuals, user stories, etc., leading to novel solutions.

- **Best Practice:** Share established methods which lead to optimal results and are often used as a benchmark, e.g. those from similar industries or competitors.

- **Prediction:** Share relevant trends or behaviors based on current data or patterns from forecasting institutes, which helps reveal a strategic direction.

- **Brainstorming:** Let the team focus on generating a broad range of ideas without immediate judgment or criticism, offering them springboards for inspiration.

- **Context:** Instruct the team to deeply consider the environment and circumstances in which the problem exists, to ensure solutions are relevant and effective.

- **Confrontation:** Actively address and discuss conflicting ideas, perspectives, or opinions within the team to resolve differences and foster innovative solutions.

- **Consensus:** Direct the team through a collaborative process, allowing all members to reach mutual agreement on a decision or solution.

- **Reflection:** Ask the individuals to think critically about their own experiences, to better understand successes and failures while spurring future improvement.

- **Voting:** Invite the individuals to express their preferences or choices in a democratic manner, then arrive at a collective decision.

Next to your chosen methods, try to consider the participants' motivations when designing the workshop. There's more than one advantage to participation and it helps you to evaluate the energy and culture of the team becoming aware of their individual motivations.

Here are several motivating factors encouraging the participants to work effectively:

- **Impact:** The participant is motivated by the desire to create meaningful and tangible changes or improvements through their design solutions.

- **Significance:** The participant is driven by the impulse to contribute to something which makes a substantial difference to their field or the wider community.

- **Expertise:** The participant is motivated by the opportunity to apply and share their specialized knowledge and skills in the design process.

- **Collaboration:** The participant is eager to work with others, combining diverse perspectives and talents to achieve a common goal.

- **Learning:** The participant wishes to acquire new knowledge, skills, and experiences through the design thinking process.

- **Higher Purpose:** The participant is driven by a goal or mission that transcends personal or immediate needs, focusing on broader, more meaningful objectives.

- **Experience:** The participant's motivation stems from the desire for a new and challenging experience which expands one's horizons and capabilities.

- **Passion:** The participant is fueled by intense enthusiasm and a deep interest in the problem at hand, driving persistent engagement.

- **Empathy:** The participant relates to the experiences, feelings, and perspectives of others, which is central to human-centered design.

Focus on Stakeholder Management

Next to selecting the lab team and designing the thinking process, involving the stakeholders from the start to the end of the project is vital.

A stakeholder is any individual, group, or organization that can affect or be affected by the outcomes of a project or decision. Stakeholders have a vested interest in a project's process and results, and can influence or be impacted by its success or failure. This includes a wide range of entities, such as employees, customers, suppliers, investors, workers' councils, community members, and even government. Understanding and managing stakeholders' expectations and needs is crucial for the initiative's success and sustainability. There are way too many expensive yet innovative solutions that were completely rejected by stakeholders after being proposed, representing a pure waste of time and money.

Stakeholders may resist change, having been used to their ways of working and thinking for decades. To complicate matters, those with power often wish to be involved in the decision-making process. Consider the so-called "innovator's dilemma". If you ask the experts, and these are usually the stakeholders and decision-makers in your organization, you'll often hear all the reasons why change shouldn't happen or why any disruptive solution will fail, because that's what usually happened in the past. Keep your eyes on the goal, letting the lab team find the solution. Involve stakeholders with care, patience, and humility right from the start. Familiarize them with the project status, asking for their opinion in interviews. Those who are curious may like to participate as silent observers at the workshop. If they're unable to participate, provide them with regular project updates and invite their feedback.

Design Thinking Works Across all Branches and Industries

With our think tank ... *and dos Santos*, we optimized the creative design process for Coca-Cola's agencies, developed a digital newspaper blueprint for Axel Springer, one of Europe's largest media publishing firms, designed the Retail Space Concept of 2028 for a major airport in Germany, and developed a new tariff option for a major mobile operator. We've developed an advanced marketing concept for a real estate platform provider, and created the go-to-market strategy for a high-tech product of Zeiss in a new market segment.

As varied as these tasks are, one impressive development isn't visible in the direct results, but in the impact on the people. Team members' collaboration with different hierarchies – of knowledge as well as power – was often unfamiliar for many at first, but led to a positive, results-rich working atmosphere. Directly combining high-ranking experts with your workforce is very inspiring and engaging. According to our customers' feedback, this often leads to more conscious decisions after the projects with greater employee involvement, coupled with a stronger team commitment. You can find more case studies of our work at anddossantos.com

Improving Innovation and Employee Happiness Through Repetition

Reflecting this positive side-effect, studies show how brain activity is stimulated through design thinking processes. People who think deeply about their own problems, are inspired by possibility, ask each other questions, develop imperatives and solutions, learn from feedback, and iterate workable solutions often undergo a rigorous personal development process. Through proposing, explaining, and questioning ideas, a deep understanding of the subject arises. Participants learn to observe and act on results derived from implementing a solution, learning from both failures and successes.

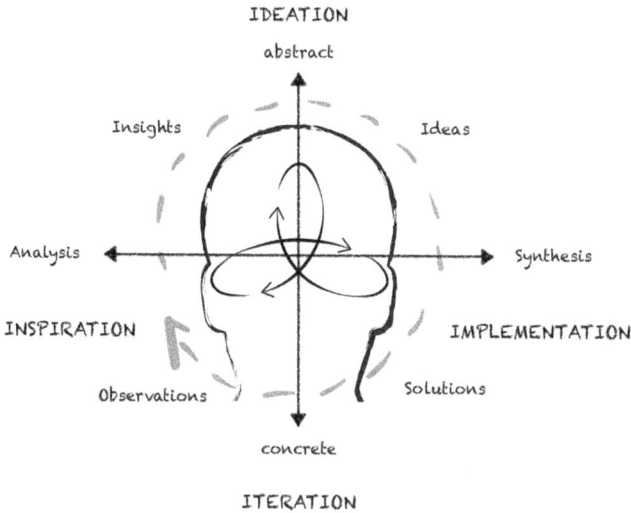

I call this effect *"brain massage"*, as the illustration above demonstrates. The four phases of the design thinking cycle stimulate different areas of the brain, thereby boosting participants' thinking capacities. The ability to collaborate, to analyze and synthesize, to consider both concrete and abstract solutions, to imagine, and to ultimately find consensus – all these steps are needed to accelerate company-wide transformation.

Step 3: The Implementation

Once the ideation workshop is complete, we develop the first rough concepts, then gather client and stakeholder feedback to sharpen them. It usually takes two to three weeks after the ideation workshop to elaborate the draft concepts, then adjust them according to overall feedback. The next stage involves preparing the successful implementation.

There are usually three major reasons why implementation fails:

- **Lack of Resources:** Often innovative solutions require notable resources, such as funding, time, or skilled personnel. If these resources are insufficient or allocated ineffectively, the solution may not be realized. This includes financial constraints, limited access to necessary technology, or manpower shortages.

- **Resistance to Change**: As mentioned repeatedly, change can be difficult for individuals and organizations alike. Employees, stakeholders, or end-users might resist new solutions due to discomfort with change, fear of the unknown, or a failure to understand the benefits. This resistance can hinder the implementation of new ideas, especially if change is perceived as disruptive or risky. That's why we focus so strongly on developing solutions from the inside out. Together with the employees, we integrate the stakeholders from start to finish and involve users in the testing process. Project management includes people management. It's important to understand the naysayers' concerns, because they simply want to protect their world from the unknown. So, help their immune system accept and understand the remedy, acknowledge the risks, and explain how you'll manage them. In my experience, when you take naysayers seriously, they let you proceed with the experiment (and often become supporters).

- **Misalignment with the Business Strategy and/or Market Needs:** Even a well-designed solution might fail if it doesn't align with the overall business strategy, objectives, or current market demands. Sometimes, solutions may be too advanced or niche, failing to meet the target market's actual needs or preferences or clashing with the organization's strategic direction or capabilities. Even if the solution is aligned with the strategy, it can fail due to the market changing more rapidly or slowly than expected. Consequently, you'd better learn to fail fast.

These challenges highlight the importance of comprehensive planning, effective resource management, change management strategies, and continuous alignment with business and market dynamics for the successful implementation of any innovative solution.

In an ideal design thinking process, you run a second workshop to prepare for proper implementation. In this implementation workshop, ideas and imperatives are worked out with the lab team, solutions are conceived, decisions and prioritizations are made, and feasibilities are considered (including the change management and communication strategy). The goal is to create a roadmap for implementation with clear to do's, responsibilities, and timeframes. In a phase following the workshop, feasibilities are evaluated in more detail and agreed with the client, based on thorough resource planning involving a detailed assessment of the required resources, including funding, technology, and personnel. You can develop a realistic budget and timeline, then secure the necessary resources in advance (including contingencies for unexpected expenses or delays). I recommend working out a comprehensive change management plan to address potential resistance, including communication strategies to ensure all stakeholders are informed and understand the innovation's benefits. Depending on the skill set of the implementation team, training and support should be provided to ease the transition. By addressing all these areas proactively, the likelihood of successfully implementing these innovative solutions can be significantly increased.

Step 4: The Iteration

When all barriers impeding implementation have been cleared, a first "MVP" (Minimum Viable Product) is developed, and the pilot testing starts. Now begins the phase of collecting feedback, followed by experimentation and learning. Then comes iteration, involving a series of attempts until the final breakthrough is achieved. (You may have to conduct a thorough risk assessment or identify further barriers impeding the implementation.) Finally, when the initial idea is manifested, it's time for celebrating!

Innovation is needed at every point in an organization, not only in product development, but in the complex area of cross-functional processes. If developed in line with the company's values, each development step offers a valuable learning experience for the team, even if success isn't achieved immediately. Adapt, learn, adapt, create. Keep transforming.

Summary of 5 Key Steps to Implement Design Thinking for a Better Tomorrow:

Step 1: Embrace Design Thinking and Collective Intelligence

Use the power of these tools to unlock creativity and innovation, boost the confidence of your team, and deliver unique solutions with the help of a *collective genius, designed* for the problem you want to solve. Design thinking is a globally proven method across various industries. Focus on the *actions* emerging from the development process, not just the ideas.

Step 2: Dedicate Your Transformation to Oneness

No matter what type of transformation your team's planning, or the problem they're aiming to solve, they should remember that oneness is the ultimate goal. Global and human wellbeing are intertwined – consider the outcome in everything you do.

Step 3: Foster Creativity and Inclusivity

Any organization that consistently applies design thinking practices out-performs others in revenues and returns. With its high strategic value, design thinking can be used to create products, strategies, processes, and many transformative solutions (including improving the employee experience). Use the power of diverse teams combining different perspectives and expertise. These are likely to be more successful, as their members complement and inspire one another.

Step 4: Ignite Collaboration

Overcome organizational resistance through emphasizing multidisci-plinary teamwork, comprehensive planning, and stakeholder engagement. Immerse yourself in empathy to understand the experiences and needs of others. Foster cross-functional collaboration, encouraging the sharing of ideas across disciplines. Manage the change process and resources well, being sensitive towards the alignment between business strategy and market needs. Advocate an iterative process, encourage the development of an MVP, and learn quickly from failures.

Step 5: Manage Stakeholder Relationships

Identify and involve stakeholders and users from the outset. Regularly update them on the project's progress and solicit their feedback.

Directing your team's thinking towards *collective genius* will generate creative and impactful outcomes. Your team's individuals will be pushed into a growth zone if you select outstanding minds. The experience will provide them with new insights and learning, higher self-esteem, and a better vision for their future. Design thinking has its limitations, but it's a valuable tool for creatively solving so-called 'wicked problems'. In addition to carefully applying the 4-step design thinking process, a well-selected and thoroughly prepared team will produce memorable results.

Engaging in design thinking processes stimulates personal and organizational growth, adaptability, and overall employee satisfaction for those who are involved in the processes or outcomes.

In the following chapter I'll outline the importance of continuous learning and new training methods. These will help you embed limitless learning within your organization, while getting the best out of human and technical development. You'll receive tools covering how to foster a shared vision and purpose for long-term growth, how to promote team learning and collaboration, and how to build a community with a growth mindset to create as many conscious leaders as possible.

CHAPTER 9

THE LEARNING CURVE

Skill development, state of mind,
and continuous evolution

"The day you stop exploring, you stop living."

— T-SHIRT SLOGAN

W hen I was thinking about how to start this chapter, I was unhappy with the quotes I'd selected for it. You shouldn't start anything with an unhappy frame of mind. So, I had a look at my dog and asked her, *"Ready for a walk?"*. We went to a small park, and I was thinking about what to cook for dinner while she was chasing a butterfly. I then saw a young man sitting on a bench. Although I'd walked at least a hundred times through this park, there had never been a man sitting on that bench before. Curious, I saw that he wore a shirt with the above slogan. I smiled.

Those who heed their sudden inspirations silence the perennial inner critic, whose appetite for perfection is insatiable. These flashes, where an idea brings immediate peace, must be cultivated. Our intuition, like any skill, improves with practice. Despite monumental advances in neuroscience, where we've explored more in the last ten years than the last hundred, the brain retains its enigmatic complexity. In particular, the prefrontal cortex – our cerebral pinnacle of evolution – allows us to manage intricate logic and introspection, enhancing social adeptness and long-term planning. When we shift into alternate states of consciousness, the prefrontal cortex partly deactivates, quieting the inner critic and letting intuition flow. Intuition isn't just mystical; it liberates us from tension and incessant inner dialogue. Creative enhancement is within our control, as is its suppression. Entering different states of consciousness through meditation, deep breathing, and mindfulness has been proven to reduce stress and improve mental health, fostering connection and existential comprehension.

Creativity Isn't Taught Like Math

If we try to teach creativity to others, we have little success. That's because creativity isn't a skill, but a state of mind. Consequently, you need to explore your own mind to find it, seeking methods that alter your consciousness. This individual journey to harness one's full capabilities demands active and conscious effort. Never stop exploring your source – it's the key to the Akashic Records, or however you like to call your unlimited access to inspiration and the universal library you can use to spark your creativity if you believe in your divine source. The world of business needs enlightened creativity to meet its complex challenges and meaningfully integrate relentless technological innovations. In response, we need new learning paradigms that expand our individual and collective consciousness.

In this chapter, I'll explain how to steadily increase your learning from the comfort zone into the growth zone, as well as how to bring consciousness to your daily learning efforts. I'll explain why not only your people's skills, but their state of mind, is key. Further, I'll outline how you can increase your learning curve and growth capacity and provide examples of how you can inspire your team to embrace limitless learning. As a 5D-Leader, you're dedicated to innovation using the latest technologies. In the great march of progress, technology first relieved our muscles, ushering us from physical toil to intellectual labor as machines took over the heavy lifting. Now, in this digital age, artificial intelligence promises a further shift, taking on the burden of our cognitive tasks. This liberation of the mind beckons us to delve deeper into the realms of emotion and empathy. As AI handles complexities, we're free to cultivate our hearts and connect more profoundly, exploring the essence of what it means to be truly human. For this reason, embrace and advance the integration of artificial and human intelligence, along with new learning systems.

New Learning Systems Balance Technological and Personal Advancement

The imperative for new, agile learning methods is driven by a rising demand for meaningful work that's in harmony with personal ethics and broader sustainability objectives. Today's workforce seeks balance, inclusivity, and diversity in the professional sphere. As organizations strive to retain top talent, they must evolve their cultures, leadership styles, and support systems to cater to the enlightened consumer whose choices are influenced by moral considerations. Technological acceleration further compounds the challenge, overwhelming resources and necessitating perpetual skill development to harness data insights, navigate digital transformations, and fortify against cyber threats. Learning strategies must be nimble and tailored, enabling immediate application of new skills. The ascendancy of AI demands a balance of soft skills with technical expertise. Navigating modern business complexities requires a culture steeped in continuous enhancement, creative resilience, and wellbeing.

"The relationship between human and artificial intelligence will eventually necessarily be one of symbiosis."

— BRYAN JOHNSON,

Tech Tycoon, CEO & Founder of KernelCo, OS Fund, Braintree

Bryan Johnson's notion that human and AI synergy is inevitable underscores our need to harness technology effectively by boosting learning agility. However, as technology prowess increases, we have to make sure our humanity doesn't decrease. And if you follow this thought, the mere replacement of human roles by AI offers no lasting edge; instead, it's the fusion of human creativity, teamwork, and introspection with AI that carves out a competitive niche. Companies ignoring AI's potential may face obsolescence, akin to those who once dismissed electricity. AI won't usurp jobs if we master the art of working alongside it. The cinematic warnings of the *Matrix* and *Terminator* scenarios implore us to embrace learning and ethical stewardship to avert a future where technology overshadows our sacred humanity.

Our brains, the most intricate constructs known, must guide us in taming creations like AI. Ethical boundaries merged with collective wisdom are essential to safeguard our prosperity.

Personal and professional development is pivotal in today's volatile world. Growth helps you become more skilled and efficient in various aspects of life, enhancing your overall performance, results, and life quality. You'll feel much better and happier as a result. As Aristotle realized, happiness is the quintessence of life; conscious learning is its conduit. Organizations nurturing employee growth don't just catalyze personal fulfillment; they lay the groundwork for professional dynamism, fostering loyalty and propelling business success. Let's dive first into the facts of learning, and why it never stops feeling uncomfortable for us.

The Uncomfortable Experience of Learning Something New

Every human is born with tremendous potential. In the process of actualizing this potential, you move through various phases. As a baby, you learn to walk because you see other humans walk, then practice until you've achieved fluid motion. You accepted falling, then just stood up again. But when you grow up, your audience's behavior changes. While your parents supported you when you failed to walk, they later became disappointed by your failures. But the metrics of learning didn't change. So, what drives our growth fastest?

A good directional guide here is our fear, because where we feel fear lies our greatest opportunity to grow. If I'm afraid of doing something that I'm reluctant to do, I see it as an invitation to open the door and discover what's behind my fear. I lean in and deal with it, and usually feel energized afterwards. I learned to accept daily discomfort as a stretch. The more I practice releasing anxiety, the more my soul enjoys becoming able to achieve a sense of flow, I observe synchronistic coincidences (you can name it luck, or a feeling supported by the universe). This keeps me going to walk the path of liberation and compassion. But I didn't start there. Progress took many painful situations and evolved through many crises. Even though I feel quite awake in my awareness today, there are throwback moments, too. Being aware of how we learn and comprehending our phases of growth helps significantly.

THE LEARNING PROCESS

In this illustration, I've split the *Learning Process* into four phases and three different levels – "How it works", "How it feels", and "What it leads to" – to explain the phases' interconnectedness.

Phase 1: Unconscious Incompetence Through Receiving Feedback

Feedback is your touchstone of reality. When you meet or surpass your expectations, that feels great. But you won't learn a lot from success. You learn fastest from your failures. Phase 1 starts with the reception of feedback that doesn't meet your expectations, or even hurts or surprises you. It works with our unconscious incompetence. We're often unaware that we can't do something, because our ego likes to think of ourselves as capable. Therefore, we need an external experience that stimulates us. Often, this emerges through failure. When working in a group, you may realize there's someone who learns faster than you. (Hello, inferiority complex, thank you for making me aware that there's an opportunity to learn!) Accept your fears, accept divine timing. Pull the fear into the light when you dislike people because of their success; don't accept your denial. Ask yourself: **What does this person do that I don't? What is there to learn?** Be yourself – you're multi-dimensional

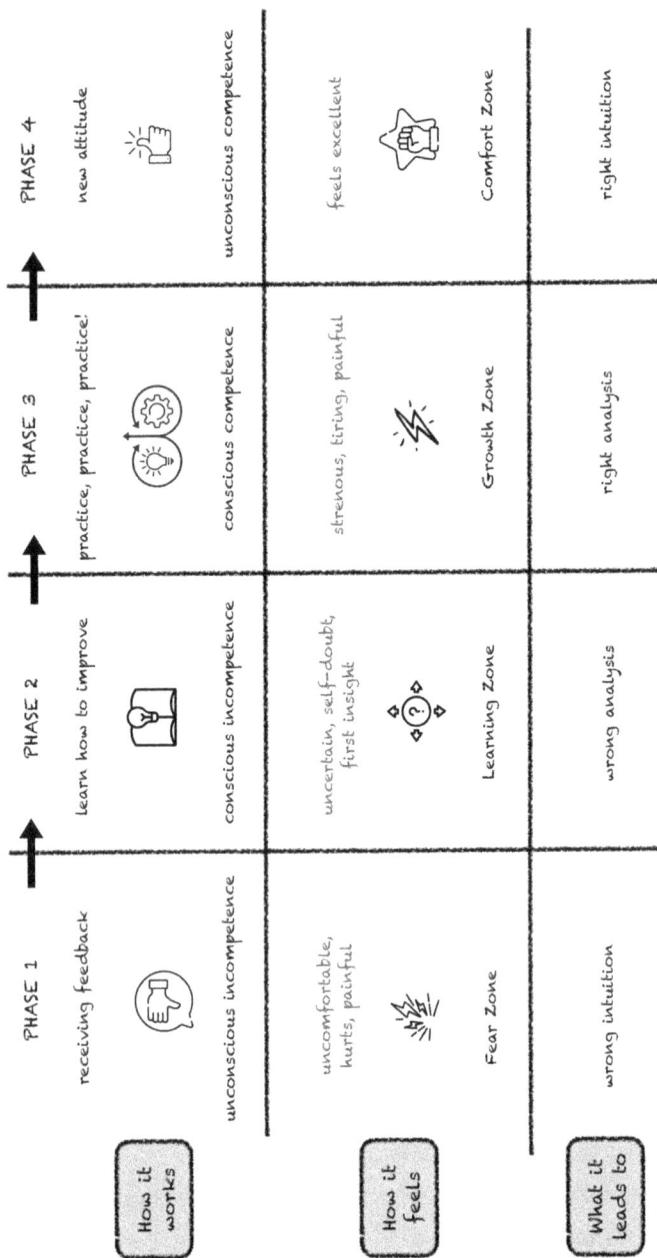

	PHASE 1	PHASE 2	PHASE 3	PHASE 4
How it works	receiving feedback unconscious incompetence	learn how to improve conscious incompetence	practice, practice, practice! conscious competence	new attitude unconscious competence
How it feels	uncomfortable, hurts, painful Fear Zone	uncertain, self-doubt, first insight Learning Zone	strenuous, tiring, painful Growth Zone	feels excellent Comfort Zone
What it leads to	wrong intuition	wrong analysis	right analysis	right intuition

and you learn in every dimension with your own tempo, sometimes fast, sometimes slowly. You'll accelerate your learning with practice.

Be conscious and watch out when listening to your intuition in low-skill areas. You're probably being led astray, because you haven't learned that area's clues yet. This is because intuition prefers the fertile ground of "unconscious competence" to be effective – but that's not Phase 1, it's the concluding Phase 4 of the Learning Process!

Don't Let Fearful Others Hold You Back

In my first role as an assistant during my early twenties at Procter & Gamble (P&G), I attended an MS Excel seminar. The next day, my fellow assistants warned me openly against making simple Excel pie charts they weren't capable of creating, fearing it would raise our bosses' expectations. Growth often faces resistance, which I'll delve into later. I insisted on utilizing my new skills to avoid wasting the company's investment in my training. While my offer to teach them was met with limited interest, I declared not to be on this planet to gratify those who want to stop me learning or trying out new things.

True contentment comes from celebrating your progress, not from denigrating others'. Accept any areas of your incompetence; it's not carved in stone. Stepping beyond comfort is daunting, requiring heightened awareness to confront fears and recognize excuses. Assess your surroundings, as they're often the chains that bind you. Growing your influence means embracing discomfort, facing the trepidation of failure, rejection, and judgment. Don't choose the safety of the known – press on instead, charting new territories.

Phase 2: Conscious Incompetence Helps You Learn to Improve

Reaching *"conscious incompetence"* is the gateway to learning how to improve. You recognize your skill gaps, and the learning journey begins. Question your awareness of what's needed, and don't hesitate to seek guidance – your self-assessment might miss the mark due to knowledge deficits. A competent mentor can shield you from missteps. Embracing the novice role, especially when adept in other domains, demands resilience but is a worthy investment. Seek out masters with a high skill level; you'll learn fastest from their immersion, and they're often generous in sharing their own uncertainties and pitfalls.

As your awareness grows and you push past familiar limits, the urge to learn intensifies. You begin to tackle problems and seize opportunities, albeit not always triumphantly, but with enough grit to gain new competencies. This evolution in consciousness is where you start crafting a vision, establishing goals, and discerning your grander mission. Being in the Learning Zone can still guide you to an incorrect analysis, because your perspective on what needs to be considered could be too narrow.

Accept Being a Beginner

Even as an expert in one area, embracing the beginner's mindset in another is vital. Mastery in one skill doesn't equate to universal proficiency. Unawareness of our skill gaps can lead to personal and professional pitfalls. Consider celebrities like athletes and actors, who excel in their crafts yet falter in personal domains like relationships or finances. Tennis legend Boris Becker faced incarceration for financial mismanagement, and Hollywood actor Johnny Depp reported a loss of over $650 million, attributing it to mismanagement by others. There are also happy heroes. Mick Jagger, pre-empting such pitfalls, studied Finance and Accounting in London to safeguard his potential rock star earnings. Unfortunately, the rags-to-riches journey is too often fraught with financial naivety; without the acumen to manage newfound wealth, even many lottery winners often face ruin a few years afterwards.

Phase 3: Conscious Competence Enters the Growth Zone

Advancing to "conscious competence" through regular practice is strenuous. Imagine the early stages of dance, when you're aware of the steps but your body hasn't quite caught up with your knowledge. As already mentioned, just like in dance, improvement in any skill comes faster with reflection and the right partners. A mirror in dance, or the guidance of a seasoned coach, helps you "mirror" others' expertise, propelling you towards your goals with accelerated learning. You may think about the movie *Shall We Dance?* with Richard Gere and Jennifer Lopez. With Lopez as your dance trainer, your motivation is raised, isn't it?

With your learning attitude now second nature, your energy frequency elevated, and your goals seemingly within reach, your confidence grows. Like an athlete visualizing their victory, you start to practice regularly and internalize new skills. You understand that interrupting or neglecting your training or the regular application of newly acquired expertise would lead to the atrophy of these skills. Masters continue to practice and usually don't like to retire. Navigating the Growth Zone takes courage; it's where you confront fears of failure, take small yet significant steps, and develop acute self-awareness to delve into life's purposes and your future vision.

Such conscious achievement heralds a mastery of anxiety and time management; it's where dreams morph into ambitious goals, self-motivation thrives, and your inner voice becomes clear, guiding you to unlock your full potential. For sure, you'll be faced with your sabotage patterns, as explained before. To reach the pinnacle of Phase 4, the journey involves deep, deliberate, and focused practice. Our brain's myelin – fatty tissue insulating neurons – increases with practice, smoothing the way for *"unconscious competence"* and the effortless expertise that crowns our efforts. This phase leads you to accurate analysis of a related situation, suggesting you've gained a broader perception.

Phase 4: Unconscious Competence Shines Through Your New Attitude

You're meant to grow as boundlessly as the cosmos. As we transition into *"unconscious competence"*, our excellence attitude shines through. Tasks become second nature, performed with an ease that amazes others. Soccer player legend Christiano Ronaldo is capable of precise headers even in the dark, which he refines not by sight but through a finely tuned sensory symphony of his trained, intuitive perception and his movement sequences, honed through intensive training. This mastery, where actions flow effortlessly, isn't just for football legends; it's attainable for all. Observe if your actions appear seamless to others, or challenge yourself to operate blindly yet proficiently. This is the joy and flow of mastery, where intuition guides us without conscious effort, honed through relentless practice – a challenging path leading to our Eden of expertise. Now you can celebrate your practice!

Excellence is Made – You are the Master of Your Learning Curve

If you don't believe that each of us is allowed to make a superhero out of ourselves, then look at the story of Maria Conceição. Growing up in poverty and losing her mother when she was two years old, Maria faced adversity from an early age. Yet she became the first Portuguese woman to summit Everest and trek to the North and South Pole, holds several Guinness World Records, has a never-give-up attitude along with the strength to constantly reinvent herself and her strategy, and believes that you can always find a path to success. On top of all that, she's an exceptional philanthropist. With no background in mountaineering, she trained for the arduous physical task of climbing Mt. Everest. With incredible endurance and sense of purpose, she learned to swim so she could cross the English Channel, raise money, continue her philanthropic work, and work toward her goal: to help transform the lives of others less fortunate. In 2005, she started an initiative in the slums of Bangladesh, where she's helped more than 600 children get an education. Among other things, she built one of the most advanced schools in Bangladesh, despite not even having completed Grade 6 herself. The determination to help others lead better lives gave Maria the energy to never give up.

Remember who you are. You're a human who deserves growth; that's your natural state. You deserve to expand naturally like the universe does. This is why those who strive for excellence never stop. They push themselves into the discomfort zone again and again until it feels like normal to them. With time, limitless learning will feel natural and easy for you.

The 7 Key Steps to Increase Your Learning Curve and Growth Capacity

Being aware of the learning phases you're in at any skill you want to improve helps you stick to the practice and overcome any sabotage pattern. Whether you want to learn a new language, arm balances in Yoga, or how to create images with AI, you need to start, learn, and experiment with your talent. Make yourself excellent. With the following seven steps, you'll pass through the different phases more easily, learning faster while having more fun.

Step 1: Continuous Learning

Always seek new knowledge and skills. This could be through formal education, self-study, online courses, or workshops. Choose which of the eleven categories of the *Life Diamond* you want to focus on, maybe one per month, and put aside a minimum of fifteen minutes daily for learning about it. Get in touch with the best players of your sport, train your intellectual capacity, or choose people with great character and read their memoirs. Don't turn on Netflix – read, learn and ignite yourself! Listen to audiobooks during exercise. Learning keeps your mind sharp and adaptable. When you learn to invest in your personal growth and collect its fruits, you'll soon learn with increased ease and happiness.

Step 2: Setting Goals

Establish clear, achievable goals for both the short and long term. Goals give direction and purpose to your efforts, phrasing them in a way that helps change your behavior. Effort feels great, at least afterwards. Get in touch with your higher self:

What achievements can you see, and what are you dreaming of? Design a colorful vision board representing how you achieved that goal or personality level. Check your goals regularly, ideally daily.

Step 3: Embracing Challenges

Step out of your comfort zone and tackle new challenges. Make this your new habit. This builds resilience and confidence, making you comfortable with looking behind your fears. But don't start with your biggest nightmares; grow your confidence little by little.

Step 4: Reflective Practice

Regularly reflect on your experiences. What did you learn? What could you do better? Reflection is key to turning experience into wisdom. You may need to quit some streaming services or your social media intake. What can you reduce to improve the time you need for yourself? Check your calendar; there's always at least a tiny space left.

Step 5: Seeking Feedback

Actively seek constructive criticism and be open to it. (Remember the *Feedback & Growth Cycle* of Chapter 3.) Feedback is a fast and crucial way of understanding how others perceive you and where you can improve. Find a community that helps you.

Step 6: Networking

Build relationships with people who inspire you, or from whom you can learn. Networking provides new perspectives and opportunities for growth. Find and build your own communities that support your growth ambitions and support you.

Step 7: Adopting a Growth Mindset

The belief that you're able to grow limitlessly is a true accelerator, so practice this. A growth mindset fosters resilience and a positive attitude towards learning and failure. Regularly check your achieved goals and learn from your failures. Use the hierarchy of the 4 Phases of the *Learning Process* to reflect on your growth.

Now let's focus on how you can inspire others as a 5D-Leader with a growth mindset. A perfect real-life example of a 5D-Leader who went through all the four phases and zones with his company and achieved a sustainable transformation is Satya Nadella, CEO of Microsoft.

Inspire an Organization to Limitless Learning and Transformation

When Satya Nadella took over Microsoft in 2014, the company was perceived as lagging behind its competitors. The organization was in the comfort zone of its established products, which were becoming less relevant in a rapidly evolving tech landscape. Nadella's journey began with moving Microsoft out of this comfort zone. He pushed the company into the fear zone by redirecting its focus to cloud computing and mobile technology, areas where Microsoft had little expertise at the time. This shift required Nadella to confront entrenched mindsets within Microsoft and the tech industry. He faced doubts and resistance but persisted, focusing on the company's learning and development.

As Microsoft entered the learning zone, Nadella emphasized the growth mindset in his book *Hit Refresh: The Quest to Rediscover Microsoft's Soul and Imagine a better Future for Everyone,* encouraging employees to see challenges as opportunities to learn and grow. He steered the company culture away from *know-it-all*, and towards *learn-it-all*.

Finally, moving into the growth zone, Microsoft saw significant success with its Azure cloud services and Office 365, regaining its position as a tech leader. Nadella's leadership exemplifies the learning curve, as he guided Microsoft through discomfort and learning to achieve new heights, reflecting both personal and organizational growth.

Not everyone has the capacity to build such extraordinary leadership skills like Satya Nadella, but he set an example of how to evolve Microsoft into a creative, open, fast-learning organization, taking his own willingness to learn and work hard as example.

How to Implement a New Learning Culture

For unlimited learning to become a matter of course for everyone in your team, and for a performance and flow-based culture of growth to emerge, I recommend the following five steps:

Step 1: Foster a Shared Vision and Purpose for Long-Term Growth

A fast way to learn about things is to teach them to others. Use these models from Comfort to Growth Zone and the *Learning Process* phases to explain to your team why it takes effort to practice. Regularly assess your skill development, ensuring that conscious learning and personal and professional growth guides them to happiness. Bring this in line with your shared company vision and purpose for growth. Remember, in Chapter 2, you defined your purpose-driven leadership. If you haven't done it yet, share this vision with your team – it will motivate them to grow with you.

People want to know why the company wants to grow, so they need to see the advantages of personal growth. Companies can't tell their employees to get into a state of flow or achieve growth. However, you can create a learning environment to pave the way.

Step 2: Ignite the Passion of Your People

Not every organization has the resources to invest in sophisticated training. There's the option of providing time for learning and experimentation, or offering a certain amount per year for any employee to participate in seminars. Companies like Google give employees *"20% time"* for passion projects, fostering innovation driven by personal vision. When you heavily invest in the autonomy and growth of your people, they'll give it back to you in surprising ways. At Google, they always prioritize employee development, providing various learning resources and opportunities; they allow employees to spend 20% of their time on personal projects they believe could benefit the business. This has led to innovations like Gmail or Google News. It's not just about providing the 20% time, because people prioritize urgent topics in their daily business. Encourage teams to develop their vision for their projects. Regularly communicate the company's overarching vision and values, showing how they align with today's and tomorrow's goals.

Step 3: Promote Team Learning and Collaboration

Coming back to the symphony of thought leaders as described in Chapter 7, we learn fast when experiencing different perspectives.

Therefore, it's vital to create interactive spaces (through office layouts or remote spaces) and opportunities for cross-departmental collaboration. The idea is to think insightfully about complex issues and develop the capacity for team members to excel collectively. Encourage multi-functional teams to reflect on successes and failures collectively; they'll then excel in solving complex problems. Using a design thinking process for this task will further improve the creativity of the team.

Personal mastery is the discipline of continually clarifying and deepening our personal vision, focusing our energies, and seeing reality objectively. Use this aspect during collaboration projects by creating room for team members to speak openly about their collective experiences. Use peer feedback as a tool, emphasizing personal growth.

Step 4: Implement Spiritual Trainings to Nurture Wellbeing

You can create individualized learning plans for employees. Offer resources, courses, and mentorship opportunities. Encourage a growth mindset, where challenges are seen as learning opportunities. Incorporate spiritual practices and teachings as part of your commitment to employee growth and wellbeing. One of the most well-known mindfulness programs is *"Search Inside Yourself"*, developed by Google engineer Chade-Meng Tan. This program was first developed in 2007 and has since gained international acclaim. It's a two-day mindfulness-based emotional intelligence training that integrates mindfulness practices, emotional intelligence concepts, and practical leadership tools. The program's goal is to help employees manage stress, improve focus, and develop empathy and resilience, thereby nurturing a more peaceful and productive work environment. Recognizing your employee growth is about more than just technical skills or knowledge. By incorporating spiritual practices and teachings, you aim to support holistic growth for personal and professional development.

In another example, Salesforce emphasizes the mental wellbeing of its employees with mindfulness zones located on every floor of their buildings. These zones are open, quiet areas where employees can meditate, relax, or simply unplug from work for a few minutes. Salesforce consistently ranks as one of the best places to work.

There's Intel's *"Intel Inside"*, an in-house mindfulness program aiming to reduce stress and increase employee happiness and creativity. A pilot program showed that participants experienced a decrease in stress and an increase in happiness and creativity, leading to the program's expansion; more companies are now starting to reduce their costs through personal wellbeing courses. Aetna International, the American healthcare company, has also implemented mindfulness and yoga programs for its employees. After running these programs, they reported a significant decrease in stress levels among participants, an average increase in productivity worth an estimated $3,000 per employee per year, and a decrease in healthcare costs.

Next to learning platforms focusing on business and technical skills, balancing human and technological growth can help your organization stay competitive and innovative in the long run and will contribute to a higher collaboration level.

Step 5: Build a Growth Mindset Community

One of the most important tasks for you as a leader is to develop the discipline to turn the mirror inward, learn to uncover our inner images of the world, bring them to the surface, and rigorously challenge them. Therefore, any growth mindset community building begins with educating yourself and thoroughly understanding the five dimensions of reality; the need to experience wholeness to strive for oneness. If you have the inner stature to drop your mask in front of others and show the willingness to develop yourself, you'll develop much faster and more easily within the circle of supportive team colleagues. Whether things work out well or go wrong, encourage questions and celebrate curiosity. The people around you will no longer be afraid to make mistakes. Mistakes shouldn't happen twice, but instead be viewed as learning opportunities. Remember to lead by example, because if you don't embody a growth mindset when you make mistakes yourself, you'll immediately lose authenticity. However, demonstrating your vulnerability will help your team grow stronger.

Building a growth community begins with a catalytic spark – a manifestation workshop can be that ignition. As a member of several such communities, I initially observed from the sidelines. In time, I engaged, sharing my narrative, voicing my fears and obstacles. This vulnerability became a pivotal moment in my personal development, affirming the value of starting anew at any stage in life. The journey deepens reciprocally – your openness encourages group depth, which in turn deepens your own insights while accelerating the emergence of your inner potential. Celebrating effort is vital; pivot from solely rewarding outcomes to valuing personal dedication and demonstrations of growth. Recognize when individuals exhibit a growth mindset, regardless of outcomes. Foster a culture of sharing –provide a hub, be it an intranet or a public domain, for exchanging resources like articles, videos, and podcasts that bolster a growth mindset, and where personal milestones can be celebrated. You're invited to join the 5D-Leadership community – sign in on glasselevator.me, and you'll receive newsletters, free activations, and invites to live events to support your limitless growth.

Conclusion

As we wrap up this chapter on the learning curve, integrating skill development, mindset, and continuous evolution, remember the mantra:

"The day you stop exploring, you stop living."

This journey began with a simple observation, a slogan on a stranger's T-shirt that sparked a smile and an inspiration, reminding us that exploration is the essence of existence. We can increase our own learning curve by being aware of the phases of learning and regularly looking for our discomfort zone instead of avoiding it. Our fear shows us the way to new insights and unlearned treasures within us. We live in such a densely connected world that we can go anywhere for help and be shown how to do something we don't yet know how to do. Learning readiness, performance delivery, and experiencing flow are closely linked; modern training techniques and online learning platforms (like Coursera, LinkedIn Learning, and many more) now enable a much less tedious way to learn new skills than was the case ten years ago based on the latest scientific research. Enable your employees to access learning, monitor progress, and establish a growth mindset community so that autonomy is created. Imagine if you could establish a community for growth in your organization, where learning and education in professional topics as well as in all areas of personal growth are supported – a community that has defined the ultimate purpose to collectively achieve *Oneness Consciousness* for humanity!

Summary of 5 Key Steps to Improve the Learning Curve

Step 1: Recognize Your Learning Process

Acknowledge where you're in the learning process. This awareness is critical to navigating through discomfort and reach mastery, accepting that excellence in one area doesn't preclude being a beginner in another. Continuous learning is vital.

Step 2: Seek Out Mentors and Coaches

Mentors and Coaches accelerate your journey from conscious incompetence to competence, sharing their expertise and reflections, helping you to break through your patterns. Enjoy the immersion of their skilled expertise and do the work. Deliberate practice builds myelin, leading to unconscious competence where skills become second nature.

Step 3: Celebrate Improvements

Shift focus from outcomes to personal growth, recognizing and valuing the learning process itself. Gamification is a true gift, helping you celebrate every little step you've made.

Step 4: Foster a Community of Growth

Cultivate a supportive environment where sharing and collaboration are encouraged, deepening personal insights and collective expertise. The deeper you go, the deeper the group goes, and the deeper the group goes, the deeper you go. That's the magic.

Step 5: Integrate Personal and Technological Development

Balance personal growth and soft skills development with technical know-how to stay competitive and innovative.

We've almost reached the end of our journey together, and I hope you're now committed to limitless learning! In the last chapter, I'll share insights into how you can sustain the spark to explore deeper into your personal growth potential, and explain why you'll experience new limits and challenges at each new level of consciousness. As you continue on the path to 5D-Leadership, I'll show you methods of dealing with your inner self-critic and self-imposed limits, through focus on your purpose and values. You'll reach new heights towards a more satisfied and fulfilled life – and through your practice, you may begin learning how to bend reality.

CHAPTER 10

SUSTAINING THE SPARK

How the elevating journey continues

"If you restore balance in your own self, you will be contributing immensely to the healing of the world."

— DEEPAK CHOPRA

P lanetary wellbeing starts with the wellbeing of yourself. With this book, I wanted to invite you to a journey that enables you to embrace your life and purposeful business challenge as a 5D-Leader with all your heart, to strengthen your spiritual roots and become aware of the different dimensions of our reality. It was my intention to inspire you to grow vertically towards reaching *Oneness Consciousness*, oneness with all living beings. I explained ways to connect your soul with your business and how to inspire your team to think more about their values, goals, and purpose to get to work with more passion, creativity, and collaboration. I highlighted the importance of taking a holistic approach to your life, with the aim of helping you make your inner *"diamond"* shine brightly and glow in the most beautiful colors of your life. This involved focusing not only on career, impact, and money, but dedicating yourself to all the valuable areas of life to experience true abundance and happiness on your own terms. Because only when we perceive ourselves holistically as human beings and bring ourselves into inner balance are we fulfilled and truly generous. It's our mastery to bring ourselves into balance and in alignment with our inner truth, and every dedicated 5D-Leader can help their teams and colleagues to recognize this path for themselves. As a result, the organization will develop positively and resourcefully. With time, this will have a positive effect on the world, in ecological, economic, and social terms. Let us all strive to reach *Oneness Consciousness.*

We must start with ourselves. In a technologically accelerating world, it's vital to firmly anchor creativity and innovation in our everyday business. For this, I've shown techniques and methods, such as forming a *collective genius* with thought leaders in your team to spark innovative ideas, foster collaboration, and get the necessary know-how and energetical support for the implementation. In addition, I showed you not only a human-centered process for solving complex problems, but also demonstrated a way to think and act more creatively and innovatively and in the last chapter, I described how to establish a growth mindset community around you – because if we share our vision, learnings, and goals with others, we can grow much faster together and support each other.

"The treasure we seek is hidden in the work we are avoiding. Understand the power of grit, if you get yourself to do the difficult things then your life becomes easier. You don't have to be perfect, the goal is positive progress, practice brings progress."

— JIM KWIK,
The World's #1 Brain Coach

Living Limitless

We all experience moments of awakening in our lives. For me, the moment I received the key to the VIP glass elevator at Sony, which I dreamed about on my very first day of work there, was such a moment. I've been reading spiritual books since I was a teenager and after three years in the Executive team of a blue-chip company, I wanted to intensify and deepen the journey towards myself. I had no idea what kind of adventure I was about to embark on; it unfolded step by step to become Co-CEO of ... *and dos Santos.* The universe has your back if you decide to live by your values and your soul. Certainly, the leap into entrepreneurship has enormously intensified my learning journey. Also, the fact that I'm married to, and work day in and day out, with the most wonderful husband of all, Ricardo, is an adventure in itself. Having created a business with and working with our amazing international and extraordinary thought leaders, who inspire me like our great clients do every day, is a true Godsend for me. One of our team members gave me the book *Limitless* by Jim Kwik, along with access to his online course. I was completely fascinated to learn how you can consciously influence your brain, massively increasing your memory or reading speed as a result, and how nutrition and exercise influence your brain capacity. I understood that the more you learn, the easier your brain keeps the memory of what you've learnt. This insight came a little late, I must admit – but the practice of forgiveness is one of the most powerful; I still must forgive myself and others every other day, as it's a great releasing practice. It's never too late to surrender, remember who you really are, and start your discovery.

THE UP-DOGS AND DOWN-DOGS OF GROWTH

Coming to the end of this book, I'd like to share with you a growth embodiment practice that motivates me to continue to go grow. With every promotion to a new role or with every big project I had to manage, there are new challenges that come along. There's never a moment when you've "arrived". Neither in a marriage, nor in a friendship, a community, a business, or in terms of your own health and finances. Yes, we can learn to hold a higher frequency of energy within us, or absorb more prana, as the yogis would say. We learn to raise our internal level of tolerance and don't accept our excuses to avoid something. When we make the connection from our head through our heart into our hands, overcoming our fears and learning to love ourselves, this experience becomes more and more intense, and the vertical journey continues.

Whether we experience *Oneness Consciousness* on this planet one day, we may never know. But for me, it's a consciousness I want to lean into and believe in, especially when I meditate with my growth community. This connectedness with like-minded people gives me infinite energy, desire and strength to strive to develop myself further into 5D-Leadership and give more of myself to helping others grow limitless.

I want to invite those who practice yoga to use the following sequence of asanas to connect with their current challenge. There's so much tension and stress you can easily solve with your breath. Regular practice leads to improvements in overall fitness and body awareness; it helps you to clear your mind and become aware of your thought patterns, which allows you to let them go. Through the movement, the asanas and conscious breathing, you feel more connected with yourself and the larger world. Through the integration of mind, body and spirit, Yoga can lead to a comprehensive evolution of the self. The following illustration does not represent a full yoga class; this flow sequence may inspire you to use these asanas to relate to current challenges in your life and grow beyond them.

The 8 Steps to Practice Growth Embodiment

Step 1: Tree Pose – Vrikshasana – Enthusiasm

When I've mastered a challenge, received a new assignment, or even experienced a proverbial promotion, then this feeling of happiness arises in me, this elation that I've done it! My imagination immediately sets in with gratitude for the new powerful "World of Being" me. I'm holding the wonderful tree pose, deeply happy and proud!

Step 2: On My Knees – Marjaryasana Bidalasana – Losing Control

I realize that I must take another step into the unknown, or perhaps many steps. Usually just a few days in the new assignment, fear rises, and I feel like losing control. Confusion and insecurities are setting in, and my confidence drops. During my corporate career, I've been promoted or changed my role more than fifteen times. Always the same stress. First, you have to say "yes" to the opportunity the university offers; then, you become afraid. The flexion and hyperextension of my spine with "cat and cow" positions keeps me flexible.

Step 3: Down-Dog – Adho Mukha Svanasana – Despair

The ups and downs are natural. When I allow my confidence to drop, despair is setting in, I'm overwhelmed with demands and dissatis-fied with my performance. Because I must do something new, I have difficulty making decisions, especially wise ones, due to the lack of knowledge and skills to make a good analysis. Whatever I start doing in the new direction, it often takes much longer than I thought. That's the Down-Dog pose for me, just deeply exhaling helps to relax! Breathe.

The 8 Steps to Practice

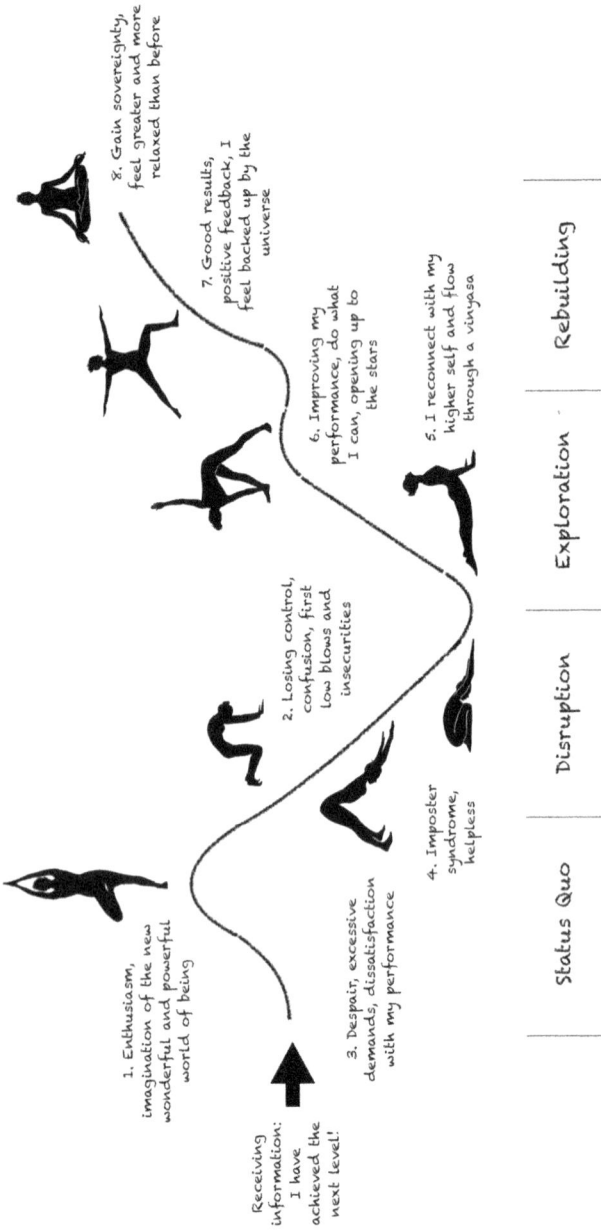

1. Enthusiasm, imagination of the new wonderful and powerful world of being

Receiving information: I have achieved the next level!

3. Despair, excessive demands, dissatisfaction with my performance

2. Losing control, confusion, first low blows and insecurities

4. Imposter syndrome, helpless

5. I reconnect with my higher self and flow through a vinyasa

6. Improving my performance, do what I can, opening up to the stars

7. Good results, positive feedback, I feel backed up by the universe

8. Gain sovereignty, feel greater and more relaxed than before

Status Quo | Disruption | Exploration | Rebuilding

Step 4: Child Pose – Balasana – Imposter Syndrome

Usually, I can't get into the new task fast enough, because the environment is unruly. If I then fail externally and internally, the *Child's Pose* helps. It disconnects me from my self-sabotaging thinking patterns. God is with me, here and now. I'm a wonderful, divine being, and I've received everything I need to master my life and this challenge. Then my gratitude and connection with my source bring me back to balance.

This is my key learning from my deepest depression. I always get from this pose into another one, come out of it through listening to myself in the silence and connect with myself, listen, and experience the insight. In this seclusion, I see again where I want to go and above all I feel that I'm still capable of acting. Time for a deep breath and for the up-dog! I feel the power in my body, the tension! With this decision to go on, maybe with a new supporter or help, things are already looking up, and even if this phase sometimes lasts longer than expected, the light at the end of the tunnel is my way to go on. Daily meditation and turning in, being grateful for the new.

Step 5: Vinyasa Flow Up-Dog – Urdhva Mukha Shavanasana – Back to Growth

I'm getting back into my flow. In each new role, there are moments when something works out well. Colleagues or clients are happy, solutions work out. As soon as something goes well, I reward myself for being brave and always ask for feedback to further improve. This is the up-dog pose, and it represents a vinyasa flow from standing to plank to down-dog to up-dog, or at least a little cobra pose.
With a flow I feel stronger, become aware of my strengths, and start to remember the moments when I feel I can connect with my higher

self, my goddess. This is the remembrance I need, and I juice up my confidence and triple my bright light emotion.

Step 6: Triangle Pose – Utthita Trikonasana – Reaching to the Stars

The goddess is within me, I've met her before, and I just remember how she feels and embody this emotion deeply. It's not yet visible on the outside, but I can feel her inside. Outside, I'm opening and reaching back to the stars, I'm improving my performance and working myself through tackling the challenges, I'm getting better.

Step 7: Warrior Pose – Virabhadrasana III – Ready to Win Again

Here I go again, standing in the warrior pose with a firm glance towards my better future! Being a warrior is wonderful and you can enjoy the pose, maybe for more than one moment. Yes, I can do it and overcome any imposter syndrome! I hold this position and embrace my future. Then, I continue with asanas and finally, I recover my resources and enjoy a deep savasana.

Step 8: Meditation – Siddhasana

My session ends by chanting an OM and finishing with a meditation in this pose. I feel one with the elements and feel how much I expanded through this practice; how great it feels!

Bending Reality

When you practice your connection with your source, work on your personal mastery, get radically responsible about your personal growth, and finally see tangible results in your reality, you still ask yourself why you are who you are, and feel small against other human giants from time to time. **The more you focus on your happiness in the now and forget about the achievements of others, the better your life gets and the faster you allow yourself to grow to the next level of your desires.**

We may look up to superhumans like Steve Jobs, J.K. Rowling, Marie Curie, Mahatma Gandhi, or Martin Luther King, who were able to dramatically change the way we perceive and interact with the world. Jobs revolutionized several industries, from personal computing to animated movies and digital publishing. J.K. Rowling transformed her life from being a single mother living on welfare to becoming one of the world's most successful and influential authors with her *Harry Potter* series. Marie Curie challenged gender norms in science and won two Nobel prizes in different scientific fields, Physics and Chemistry. Mahatma Gandhi used nonviolent resistance to lead the successful campaign for India's independence from British rule, and King was instrumental in the American Civil Rights movement which transformed American society. Superhumans seem to bend reality and leave a dent in our universe. *"Bending reality"* is a metaphorical concept used to describe how people, without altering physical reality, can change one's perception and interaction with the world and achieve extraordinary results. What can we learn from this? Think bold.

Cultivate a mindset that embraces possibilities rather than limitations, practice visualizing your successes and achieving your goals, imagine the process and your incredible results vividly. Understand your failures as learning opportunities and stepping stones to your success and develop the resilience to bounce back from setbacks and keep pushing forward. Build relationships and a community around you that offer you different perspectives to grow. When you realize that your dreams can come true, and you get more and more aware that you can make them come true (like when I experienced my first ride with the VIP glass elevator at Sony, which I had as a dream in my mind for two years from the moment I entered the building for the first time), you can describe this moment as bending reality. It's not about how big your achievement is, or how impactful or prominent you are. It's all about how it feels for yourself, and how you can increase your contribution through your purposeful work, through your dedication to become the best version of yourself every day.

"This is the true joy in life, the being used for a purpose recognized by yourself as a mighty one. The being thoroughly worn out before you are thrown on the scrap heap; the being a force of Nature instead of a feverish selfish little clod of ailments and grievances complaining that the world will not devote itself to making you happy.

I am of the opinion that my life belongs to the community, and as long as I live, it is my privilege to do for it whatever I can. I want to be thoroughly used up when I die, for the harder I work, the more I live. Life is no "brief candle" to me. It is a sort of splendid torch which I have got hold of for a moment, and I want to make it burn as brightly as possible before handing it on to the future generations."

— GEORGE BERNARD SHAW

Altered States

In the last chapter, I mentioned altered states of consciousness that allow you to access flow states or intuitive insights. Altering one's state of consciousness can be achieved through various means, some of which are natural and safe, while others involve substances that may have legal and health implications, like plant medicine. Approach this topic with caution, prioritizing safety and wellbeing, as the use of certain substances are subject to legal restrictions. There are natural and safe techniques like meditation or guided visualizations that can induce altered states of consciousness, leading to deep relaxation, heightened awareness, or profound insights. Also, Breathwork techniques like Holotropic Breathwork or Pranayama can significantly alter your state of consciousness, creating experiences of deep emotional release or spiritual awakening; there are numerous teachers and online courses practicing it. You may prefer to use float tanks where you float in a dark, soundproof tank filled with saltwater, which can induce a deeply relaxed state and alter your sensory experience. Since you're an individual, you need to experiment with which technique responds to you. I love hypnosis, e.g. with Paul McKenna or Marisa Peer. They offer hypnotherapeutic courses and allow me deep relaxation, aiding me through suggestions in my behavior change and emotional healing. Other techniques include Lucid Dreaming, where through creating vivid and controllable dream experiences, you're led to profound personal insights and creativity. Last but not least are Yoga and Tai Chi, which bring body, mind, and spirit in harmony through practice.

I learned to concentrate better by listening to binaural beats. These audio tracks can influence brainwave patterns, leading to improved focus or altered states of consciousness. Technology offers many new learning experiences. With the expansion of augmented and virtual reality, we can alter our perception of reality and induce unique states of consciousness, especially in more advanced, interactive environments involving all our senses. There are researchers working on learning injections like in the *Matrix* movies to influence our brain rapidly. For more natural methods, such as psychedelics like ayahuasca or deep meditation retreats, having professional guidance and support is crucial. Remember, they work differently for each person. What leads to an altered state for one may not have the same effect on another.

Final Words

As we conclude this journey, let's cherish your *Life Diamond*, shining with your true values and aspirations. This path of 5D-Leadership isn't a destination, but a call to continual growth and purposeful living. In the dance of growth, each breath and pose fortifies your resolve. Remember, true greatness lies in your authentic steps and the belief in your potential. And don't forget, life is not about the destination or the journey, but the company we experience. Choose your company wisely.

Let this book be your guide, inspiring creativity amidst technological advances. Embrace the *collective genius*, transforming ideas into tangible outcomes; now, take the leap. Engage in practices like meditation to weave your part in our collective consciousness. And as you move forward, bring the light of learning and love for community with you.

The treasure is in the challenges we face. Step into your arena and carve your legacy. Rise as a 5D-Leader, molding reality with passion and purpose. Let's march towards a brighter future, where your spark leads the way for humanity.

On glasselevator.me/5D-Leadership, you'll find more advanced advice and free information and activations. You can subscribe to my newsletter, join the community, or book online courses or live events that will take you further on your journey. I wholeheartedly wish you success and much joy on this adventure. I look forward to your personal feedback at mail@glasselevator.me

JOIN THE 5D-LEADERSHIP COMMUNITY

Thank you for sharing your awareness with *The Glass Elevator*. I extend a heartfelt invitation to you, the visionary leaders who have traversed these pages alongside me. Thank you so much for exploring the depths of 5D-Leadership, a new paradigm that champions unity, collaboration, and transformation, underpinned by living your life to the fullest.

The principles of 5D-Leadership, as laid out in this book, shall serve as your guide, inspiring you towards fostering environments where oneness isn't just an esoteric ideal, but a living, breathing reality. Let's transcend traditional boundaries and embrace a holistic vision that benefits all stakeholders: employees, customers, communities, and the planet.

The journey, however, doesn't end here. It's one thing to understand the principles of 5D-Leadership; it's another to live them, to do the work daily, to measure your progress, and to celebrate! To weave the principles into the fabric of your organizations, and to inspire those around you to do the same. This is why I'm inviting you to join the

5D-Leadership Community – a network of like-minded leaders committed to driving positive change.

By joining the 5D-Leadership Community, you'll gain access to a supportive network of peers and a wealth of resources designed to aid your continuous growth as a conscious leader.

We're offering inspiring webinars and ongoing opportunities for learning and newsletters.

Your insights, experiences, and leadership will enrich this community, just as you'll be enriched by the collective wisdom it holds. As you turn this final page, consider it not an end but a beginning. The start of a new chapter in your leadership journey, one that promises not only personal transformation but the potential to shape a more compassionate, collaborative, and sustainable world. Join us.

Together, we can ascend as architects of a brighter future.

Welcome aboard the glass elevator!

With deepest gratitude,

Yours, Jutta

glasselevator.me/5D-Leadership

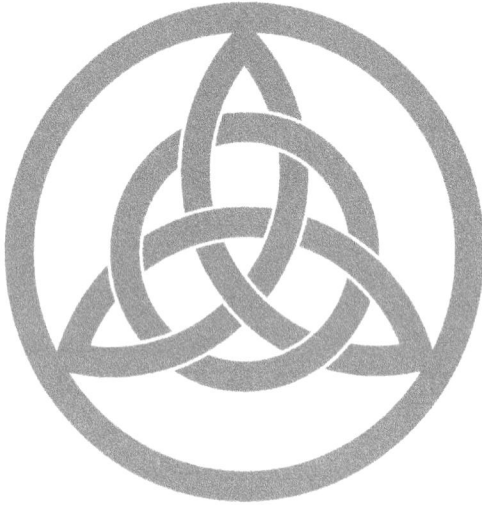

THE QUINTARA

As part of your journey with the 5D-Leadership Community, you'll also come to recognize our symbol, a refined triquetra with dual concentric circles. This emblem represents the unity and diversity fundamental to our ethos. The triquetra, an ancient symbol of interconnectedness and balance among the trio of earth, water, and fire, or divinity in its many forms, is enfolded by an inner circle that symbolizes wholeness and infinity. A larger encompassing circle radiates outward, representing our shared pursuit of one consciousness. The Quintara, our emblem, not only reminds us to harmonize the spiritual with the material and the individual with the collective but also stands as a profound symbol of diversity and the sense of belonging that unites us on our journey to oneness.

SOURCES

BEHIND THE WORDS

1. **Witherspoon,** Reece (*Glamour* 2015, November 11). *Women of the Year Award Speech [Video file].* YouTube https://youtu.be/GnCk5YbzAVQ
2. **Jung,** Carl. *Worte der Seele.* Herder, 1995.
3. **Dalai Lama.** *Das Herz aller Religionen ist eins.* Hoffmann & Campe, 1997.
4. **Wilber,** Ken. *Wege zum Selbst.* Kösel, 1991.
5. **State of the Global Workplace Report,** Gallup Inc. 2023, https://www.gallup.com/workplace/349484/state-of-the-global-workplace.aspx
6. **Paramahansa,** Yogananda. *Autobiography of a Yogi.* Self-Realization Fellowship, 1974.
7. **Teilhard de Chardin,** Pierre (2024, April 25). In *Wikipedia.* https://en.wikipedia.org/wiki/Pierre_Teilhard_de_Chardin

INTRODUCTION

1. **Bin Rashid Al Maktoum,** Mohammed (2024, April 25). In *Wikipedia.* https://en.wikipedia.org/wiki/Mohammed_bin_ Rashid_Al_Maktoum#:~:text=He%20oversaw%20the%20 growth%20of,are%20held%20by%20Dubai%20Holding

2. **Ma,** Jack (2024, April 25). In *Wikipedia.* https://de.wiki-pedia.org/wiki/Jack_Ma

3. **Ma,** Jack (2024, July 25), Love is important in business. *World Economic Forum, 2018* http://www.youtube. com/watch?v=4zzVjonyHcQ

CHAPTER I

1. **Al Madani,** Sarah. *Your brain is like tofu (2024, April 25) [Video file].* YouTube. https://www.youtube.com/watch?v=cF1ARQNfAt4

2. **Maslow,** Abraham. *Hierarchy of Needs (2024, April 25).* In *Wikipedia.* https://en.wikipedia.org/wiki/Maslow%27s_ hierarchy_of_needs

3. **Kumari,** Gargi (2021, February 2). *LinkedIn: From a Career Portal to the World's Biggest Professional Network.* The Strategy Story. https://thestrategystory.com/2021/02/02/ linkedin-growth-story/

4. **Laloux,** Frederic. *Reinventing Organizations.* Nelson Parker, 2014.

5. **Lee,** William (1999). *A Comparison of the Spiral Dynamic Map with Other Maps.* Dr Clare W. Graves Research. https://www.clarewgraves.com/research_content/CG_others/intro.html

6. **van Lente,** Erik (2020). *Understanding the Nature of Oneness Experience in Meditators Using Collective Intelligence Methods.* Frontiers in Psychology 11, 17 September. https://www.frontiersin.org/journals/psychology/articles/10.3389/fpsyg.2020.02092/full

7. **Weiner,** Jeff (2020, September 3). *Leading Like a CEO [Video file].* LinkedIn. https://www.linkedin.com/learning/jeff-weiner-on-leading-like-a-ceo/welcome-to-leading-like-a-ceo

8. **Wilber,** Ken. *The Integral Vision: A Very Short Introduction.* Shambala Publications Inc., 2007.

CHAPTER 2

1. **Butcher,** John. *Lifebook Program (2024, April 25).* Mindvalley. https://www.mindvalley.com/lifebook

2. **Mother Theresa** (2024, April 25). In *Wikipedia.* https://en.wikipedia.org/wiki/Mother_Teresa

3. **Chouinard,** Yvon (2024, April 25). *Website.* https://www.patagonia.com/ownership/

4. **Rumi** (2024, April 25). In *Wikipedia.* https://de.wikipedia.org/wiki/Rumi_(Dichter)

5. **Sorenson,** Susan (2013, June 20). *How Employee Engagement Drives Growth.* Gallup Business Journal, https://www.dyckerhoff-bdu.de/images/Downloads/Dyckerhoff_Gallup_Studie_How%20_Employee_Engagement_Drives_Growth.pdf

CHAPTER 3

1. **Rowling,** Joan (2011, September 16). *J.K. Rowling Speaks at Harvard Commencement [Video file].* YouTube. https://www.youtube.com/watch?v=wHGqp8lz36c
2. **Winfrey,** Oprah (2013, May 30). *Oprah Winfrey Harvard Commencement Speech [Video file].* YouTube. https://www.youtube.com/watch?v=GMWFieBGR7c
3. **Robbins,** Tony *(n.d.).* *Author Website.* https://www.tony-robbins.com/

CHAPTER 4

1. **Barrett,** Richard. *The Values-Driven Organization: Unleashing Human Potential for Performance and Profit.* Routledge, 2013.
2. **Brown,** Brené (2010, December). *The Power of Vulnerability [Video file].* TED Conferences. https://www.ted.com/talks/brene_brown_the_power_of_vulnerability
3. **Diamandis,** Peter & **Ismail,** Salim. *Exponential Organizations (Book 2.0).* Ethos Collective, 2023.
4. **Diamandis,** Peter & **Kotler,** Steven. *The Future is Faster Than You Think.* Simon & Schuster, 2020.

5. **Hamel,** Gary & **Zanini,** Michelle. *Humanocracy: Creating Organizations as Amazing as the People Inside Them.* Harvard Business Review Press, 2020. Bureaucratic Mass Index: https://www.humanocracy.com/course/BMI

6. **Laloux,** Frederic. *Reinventing Organizations.* Nelson Parker, 2014.

7. **Singh,** Harmit (2022, February 18). *4 Lessons from Levi's Digital Transformation.* Harvard Business Review, https://hbr.org/2022/02/4-lessons-from-levis-digital-transformation

8. **Global Data Creation is About to Explode** (2019, April 16). In Statista. https://www.statista.com/chart/17727/global-data-creation-forecasts/

CHAPTER 5

1. **Benioff,** Marc (2024, April 25). In *Wikipedia.* https://en.wikipedia.org/wiki/Marc_Benioff

2. **Johansson,** Frans & **Hastwell,** Claire (2022). *Why Diverse and Inclusive Teams are the Engines of Innovation.* Great Place to Work, https://www.greatplacetowork.com/resources/blog/why-diverse-and-inclusive-teams-are-the-new-engines-of-innovation

3. **Brind-Woody,** Claudia (2024, April 25). *Home [LinkedIn page].* https://www.linkedin.com/in/claudia-brind-woody/

4. **Oura** (2024, April 25). *Smart Ring for Fitness, Stress, Sleep & Health.* https://ouraring.com

5. **Winfrey,** Oprah (2013, May 30). *Oprah Winfrey Harvard Commencement Speech [Video file].* YouTube. https://www.youtube.com/watch?v=GMWFieBGR7c

CHAPTER 6

1. **Richmond,** Jason (2024, April 25). *The Employee And Customer Experience: What Do They Have In Common?.* Forbes Business Council, Council Post. https://www.forbes.com/sites/forbesbusinesscouncil/2022/07/21/the-employee-and-customer-experience-what-do-they-have-in-common/

2. **Branson,** Richard (2024, April 25). *Richard Branson's Blog.* https://www.virgin.com/branson-family/richard-branson-blog

3. **Edmeades,** Eric (2024, July 25). *Business Freedom Blueprint. Mindvalley.* 2022 https://www.mindvalley.com/freedom

4. **Ferrazi,** Keith. *Leading Without Authority: How the New Power of Co-Elevation Can Break Down Silos, Transform Teams, and Reinvent Collaboration.* Crown, 2020.

5. **Hsieh,** Tony. *Delivering Happiness: A Path to Profits, Passion, and Purpose.* Grand Central Publishing, 2011.

6. **Sinek,** Simon (n.d.). Author Website. https://simonsinek.com/

7. **Covey,** Steven R. (2024, April 25). In *Wikipedia.* https://de.wikipedia.org/wiki/Stephen_R._Covey

CHAPTER 7

1. **Catmull,** Ed. *Creativity, Inc.* Bantam, 2014.

2. **Lévy,** Pierre (2024, April 25). In *Wikipedia.* https://en.wikipedia.org/wiki/Pierre_L%C3%A9vy

CHAPTER 8

1. **Bender-Salazar,** Rahmin (2023). *Design thinking as an effective method for problem-setting and needfinding for entrepreneurial teams addressing wicked problems.* Journal of Innovation and Entrepreneurship 12(24), 1–23. https://www.researchgate.net/publication/369977663_Design_thinking_as_an_effective_method_for_problem-setting_and_needfinding_for_entrepreneurial_teams_addressing_wicked_problems

2. **Cleveland Clinic** (2024, April 25). *The Human Connection to Patient Care [Video file]. YouTube.* https://www.youtube.com/watch?v=cDDWvj_q-o8

3. **Christensen,** Clayton. *The Innovator's Dilemma: When New Technologies Cause Great Firms to Fail.* Harvard Business Press, 2016.

4. **Kelley,** David M. (2024, April 25). In *Wikipedia.* https://en.wikipedia.org/wiki/David_M._Kelley

5. **Lewrick,** Michael. *The Design Thinking Playbook.* Wiley, 2018.

6. **Lewrick,** Michael. *The Design Thinking Toolbox.* Wiley, 2020.

7. **Sheppard,** Benedict (2018, October 25). *The Business Value of Design.* McKinsey Quarterly. https://www.mckinsey.com/capabilities/mckinsey-design/our-insights/the-business-value-of-design/

CHAPTER 9

1. **Johnson,** Brian (2016, October 20). *Kernel's Quest to Enhance Human Intelligence.* Medium. https://bryan-johnson.medium.com/kernels-quest-to-enhance-human-intelligence-7da5e16fa16c
2. **Nadella,** Satya. *Hit Refresh: The Quest to Rediscover Microsoft's Soul and Imagine a Better Future for Everyone.* Harper Collins, 2017.
3. **da Conceição,** Maria (2024, April 25). *Maria da Conceição.* Author website. https://www.mariadaconceicao.com/

CHAPTER 10

1. **Kwik,** Jim. *Limitless: Upgrade Your Brain, Learn Anything Faster, and Unlock your Exceptional Life.* Hay House Inc., 2020.
2. **Shaw,** George Bernard (2024, April 25). In *Wikipedia.* https://de.wikipedia.org/wiki/George_Bernard_Shaw
3. **Peer,** Marisa. *Author website.* https://marisapeer.com/
4. **McKenna,** Paul. *Author website.* https://www.paulmckenna.com/

RECOMMENDATIONS

1. **Alexander,** Valerie. *How Women Can Succeed in the Workplace (Despite Having 'Female Brains').* Goalkeeper Media, 2014.
2. **Brown,** Brené. *Daring Greatly: How the Courage to Be Vulnerable Transforms the Way We Live, Love, Parent, and Lead.* Portfolio Penguin, 2013.
3. **Brown,** Brené. *Braving the Wilderness.* Random House, 2017.
4. **Campbell,** Bill. *Trillion Dollar Coach [Audiobook].* Harper Audio, 2019.
5. **Carnegie,** Dale. *How to Win Friends and Influence People.* Pocket Books, 2010.
6. **Chopra,** Deepak & **Kafatos,** Menas. *You are the Universe: Discovering your Cosmic Self and Why it Matters.* Ebury Digital, 2017.
7. **Chopra,** Deepak. *The Seven Spiritual Laws of Success.* Transworld Publishers, 1996.
8. **Chopra,** Deepak. *The Ultimate Happiness Prescription.* Rider, 2017.
9. **Clear,** James. *Atomic Habits.* Penguin, 2018.

10. **Cotton,** Michael. *Source Code Meditation: Hacking Evolution Through Higher Brain Activation.* Findhorn Press, 2018.
11. **Coyle,** Daniel. *The Culture Code: The Secrets of Highly Successful Groups.* Random House, 2018.
12. **Dalai Lama.** *Das Buch der Menschlichkeit.* **Bastei Lübbe,** 2000.
13. **Diallo,** Ray. *Principles: Life and Work.* Simon & Schuster, 2017.
14. **Doerr,** John. *Measure What Matters.* Penguin, 2018.
15. **Grant,** Adam. *Think Again.* Penguin, 2021.
16. **Gray,** John. *Männer sind anders, Frauen auch: Männer aind vom Mars, Frauen von der Venus.* Goldmann, 1993.
17. **Hamel,** Gary. *Das Ende des Managements: Unternehmensführung im 21. Jahrhundert.* Ullstein, 2007.
18. **Hicks,** Esther. *The Law of Attraction.* Hay House, 2006.
19. **Hillyer,** Regan & **Barahona,** Juan Pablo. *The Abundance Codes: Fifty-Two Codes to Unlock Abundance in Every Area of Your Life.* Lion Crest, 2019.
20. **Horowitz,** Ben. *The Hard Things About Hard Things [Audiobook].* Harper Audio, 2014.
21. **Isaacson,** Walter. *Elon Musk.* Simon & Schuster, 2023.
22. **Jeevan,** Sharath. *Intrinsic: A Manifesto to Reignite Your Inner Drive.* Endeavour, 2021.
23. **Jobs,** Steven (2005, June 12). *Steve Jobs' 2005 Stanford Commencement Address [Video file].* YouTube. https://www.youtube.com/watch?v=UF8uR6Z6KLc
24. **Kofman,** Fred. *Conscious Business.* Sounds True, 2006.

25. **Kotler,** Steven. *Stealing Fire: How Silicon Valley, the Navy SEALS, and Maverick Scientists are Revolutionizing the Way We Live and Work.* Dey Street Books, 2017.
26. **Lakhiani,** Vishen. *The Buddha and the Badass: The Secret Spiritual Art of Succeeding at Work.* Rodale Books, 2020.
27. **Lakhiani,** Vishen. *The Code of an Extraordinary Mind: 10 Unconventional Laws to Redefine Your Life and Succeed on Your Own Terms.* Rodale Books, 2016.
28. **Lim,** Jenn. *Beyond Happiness: How Authentic Leaders Prioritize Purpose and People for Growth and Impact.* Hachette Book Group, 2021.
29. **Loehr,** Jim & **Schwartz**, Tony. *On Form: Managing Energy, Not Time, is the Key to High Performance, Health and Happiness.* Nicholas Brealey Publishing, 2008.
30. **Mackey,** John & **Sisodia**, Rajendra. *Conscious Capitalism: Liberating the Heroic Spirit of Business.* Harvard Business Review Press, 2012.
31. **McCord,** Patty. *Powerful: Building a Culture of Freedom and Responsibility.* Silicon Guild, 2018.
32. **Reinhardt,** Kai. *Digitale Transformation der Organisation: Grundlagen, Praktiken und Praxisbeispiele der digitalen Unternehmensentwicklung.* Springer Gable, 2020.
33. **Rosling,** Hans. *Factfulness: Ten Reasons We're Wrong About The World – And Why Things Are Better Than You Think.* Sceptre, 2018.
34. **Schucman,** Dr Helen. *A Course in Miracles, Foundation For Inner Peace 2017 (Book & online course).* https://acim.org/acim/en

35. **Shaw,** Robert. *Extreme Teams: Why Pixar, Netflix, Airbnb, and Other Cutting-Edge Companies Succeed Where Most Fail [Audiobook].* Brilliance Audio, 2017.

36. **Smothermon,** Ron. *Das Mann/Frau Buch,* Kamphausen, 1998.

37. **Smothermon,** Ron. *Drehbuch für Meisterschaft im Leben.* Kamphausen, 1996.

38. **Tolle,** Eckehart. *Jetzt! Die Kraft der Gegenwart.* Kamphausen, 2010.

39. **Tolle,** Eckehart. *Eine Neue Erde: Bewusstseinssprung Anstelle von Selbstzerstörung.* Arkana, 2015.

ACKNOWLEDGEMENTS

I want to say thank you to the following people:

Ricardo, for believing in this project for so many years, and for believing in me even longer. Thank you so much for your love, for offering the space to focus on my passion, and for helping me to move on when I was exhausted. I especially thank you for using your enthusiasm for diversity and design to make Collective Intelligence Design the core model of ... *and dos Santos* and for taking me on this journey with you. I look forward to our continued expansion and the future that lies ahead.

My mother, for sharing her life with authors and making me feel worthy.

My sister, whom I admire for her unlimited passion for arts, history, and traveling, is always in my heart. Though she left us too soon, losing her battle to cancer, her spirit continues to inspire me every day. I miss her dearly and keep her memory alive within me forever.

Without you, this book wouldn't exist:

To our creators at ... *and dos Santos:* Valerie Alexander, Kamil Banc, Ryatoro Bordini Chikushi, Prof. Dr. Regina Cordes, Andreas Dittes, Ralf Echtler, Achim Feige, Jan Fiedler, Andreas Gebhard, Richard Godfrey, Ronen Kadushin, Marina Löwe, Severin Matusek, Harald Melwisch, Rahel Morgen, Prof. Dr. Marc Opresnik, Dagmar Pithan, Adina Popescu, Stefanie Salata, Prof. Dr. Christian W. Scheiner, Leah Stuhltrager, Katrin J. Yuan and our friend and advisor Dirk Boettcher.

To my inspirations and supporters for this book – Swantje Steinbrink, Pegah Gol, Clare McIvor and Moustafa Hamwi and the whole Passionpreneur team, your assistance was incredible and amazing. To Achim Daub, Norbert Koll, Sanna Suvanto-Harsaae, Sylke Fleischhut, Martin Winkler, Jaap Koopmans, Oliver Kaltner, Mary Carethers and Christian Bremicker for your memorable leaderships advice and to Josephine Ackerman and Matthias Kellersohn for your trust and passion to change and grow.

To my wonderful, empowered goddesses Jasmina Hirschmann, Sarah Perings, Friederike (Sadhana) von Benten, Hanna Oberkersch and to Regan Hillyer, Vishen Lakhiani, and Claudia Schiffer. Immense gratitude to my dearest friends Ute Zahn and Mario Gallasch for always standing by my side and infinite thanks to all my beloved relatives, closest friends, incredible clients, and our greatest team of all time.

ABOUT THE AUTHOR

Jutta is a visionary, award-winning entrepreneur and co-CEO of ... *and dos Santos*, with a prolific background spanning over twenty-five years in leadership, corporate culture, and consulting.

Her career is marked by an unwavering commitment to innovation and transformative change, both within the workplace and in broader societal contexts.

Jutta's expertise lies in her ability to intertwine digital innovation with human-centric values, fostering environments where creativity, happiness, and diversity are not just encouraged but valued as foundational principles.

At the heart of Jutta's work is the innovative concept of collective intelligence, which has revolutionized the way companies approach digital and cultural transformation. Through ... *and dos Santos*, Jutta has played a pivotal role in guiding prestigious clients like Deutsche Bahn, L'Oréal, Olympus, Red Bull, and Zeiss towards groundbreaking achievements by harnessing the power of collective wisdom.

Jutta's professional journey commenced at P&G Prestige Beauté, where she launched acclaimed brands such as Boss Woman and Helmut Lang in the DACH region. Her career trajectory took her to Storck and Sony, where she excelled in driving behavioral and digital change as well as in global project management, operational restructuring, and new business development, always with a keen focus on digital innovation and fostering individual growth of her employees and international team elevation.

She lives in Berlin with her husband Ricardo (the founder and co-CEO of ... *and dos Santos*) and their Dalmatian dog Luísa.

Jutta is a member of the Berlin Chamber of Commerce Parliament and supports transformative organizations such as Global Goals Berlin, which aims to promote and implement the United Nations Sustainable Development Goals at the local level in Berlin.

NOTES

THE GLASS ELEVATOR

....

....

....

....

....

....

....

....

....

....

....

NOTES

....

....

....

....

....

....

....

....

....

....

....

....

....

THE GLASS ELEVATOR

....

....

....

....

....

....

....

....

....

....

....

....

www.ingramcontent.com/pod-product-compliance
Lightning Source LLC
Chambersburg PA
CBHW031842200326
41597CB00012B/236